HERITAGE
from
FATHER

Healing Genocide Wounds through Gratitude and Faith

HORMISDAS NDAYISHIMIYE

BALBOA.
PRESS
A DIVISION OF HAY HOUSE

Balboa Press books may be ordered through booksellers or by contacting:

Balboa Press
A Division of Hay House
1663 Liberty Drive
Bloomington, IN 47403
www.balboapress.com
1 (877) 407-4847

Printed in the United States of America.

ISBN: 978-1-4525-8365-5 (sc)
ISBN: 978-1-4525-8366-2 (e)

Balboa Press rev. date: 02/11/2014

To my parents, Siméon and Odette; my brothers and sisters François, Antoine, Emile, Michel, Bernadette, and Marthe. You were killed by people who had lost faith in God. I will never forget your love, and I do believe that, where you are in heaven, you keep praying for me to prevent me from indulging in ingratitude or straying away from faith.

To my brothers Alexis, Alexandre, and Godefroid. Sharing the heritage from Father makes our lives stronger.

To my new family, Marie-Claire, Davina, and Anaïs. Your love and support are necessary to help me stay connected with the source of my being.

To the victims of genocide all over the world and to all those with wounds from injustice and other ills in this world.

All this is obviously easy to understand. We all know that we shall be grateful if we are aware of the favor bestowed on us.

—Luiz, Jean Lauand

CONTENTS

PREFACE

This book tells a true story: the story of my family, the story of myself. But it's also a story of miracles, faith, compassion, love, and gratitude. It is also a story of the horror of genocide and its utmost cruelty.

This book would not have been written if I had not been bound to constant gratitude toward God for my survival and my psychological and spiritual healing. These blessings bestowed upon me urged me to share my experience with Rwandan people and the world at large in a bid to put in place a culture of gratitude, particularly as a healing option for a society under trauma. My book pretends to open up this unexplored but instrumental perspective for other societies in a world that is increasingly racked by innumerable divisions and their fate of hate and ingratitude.

In the narrative, I cited people's names only when I found it necessary for the common good rather than for anyone's propaganda. However, I changed the names of a number of individuals to protect their private lives. I believe that the source of my life is the same as other people's lives. With *Heritage from Father*, I wish to share my experience with many people in the hope that the values that healed me will be of assistance to other people in the world.

REMEMBERING GOD'S BLESSINGS

My parents and six brothers and sisters had been just killed—not by accident or an unspecified epidemic but by their extremist Hutu neighbors. They were killed because of their identity; they were called Tutsis. April 1994: The media all over the world were about the hunting of the Tutsis. The genocide against this group of people had started in Rwanda. I was completely demoralized, upset, bitter, and angry. I wished God could unleash lightning upon all the Hutus. I was overcome with revenge and was at a loss for what to do. I was very far from my home country in Messina, which is located in the Italian province of Sicily. I was the only Rwandan national in that locality, possibly in all of Sicily, and was looking for someone with whom to talk about the horror in my Kinyarwanda mother tongue, and I could not find anyone. I was almost insane, talking to myself aloud. I was gesticulating, enacting someone firing at people. I was entirely possessed by hatred.

I had no respite, day and night. During the day, I felt like waging war against myself, trying to imagine my relatives' suffering before they were killed. At night, I could not find sleep and was tormented by nightmares. Two whole weeks went by without ceasefire. Fortunately, as he had always assisted me in hard times,

God sent someone to call me to remember the comforting kindness I had received in my great painful moments. In an agreeable way, the Godsend messenger reminded me that my father had advised me to practice constant gratitude and had often warned me against hatred. I remembered that since 1990, I had started praying day and night for God to give me an opportunity of leaving my country that had started killing its own people. I remembered that in 1992, my prayers were answered when God let me out of Rwanda, probably to save me from the horror. I noted that in spite of everything, I survived where my relatives had been killed. Then I started wondering what price I had paid to be in a peaceful foreign country while my home country was the scene of genocide.

I kept remembering. I remembered that I had been raised by my parents while some of my countrymen had been orphaned since 1959, when the Tutsis were first hunted down. I also remembered that in 1963, the year of my birth, the killings of the Tutsis were so widespread and systematic that a few reporters linked them to some sort of genocide. I remembered that my father had given me a name of gratitude toward God, a sign of recognition that he had survived those periods of persecution by a hair's breadth.

When I meditated, especially on these blessings, my unhappiness vanished, and I saw myself in a new light: I was privileged compared to the many Rwandans who had faced death. Thank God! I resolved that hatred should in no way find a place in my being. I was to fight it with all my heart and soul.

As I gradually fought against hatred, anger, resentment, and the spirit of revenge, God multiplied his miracles in my favor through Sicilian people in particular and the Italians in general. I was able to find the love and compassion I had been deprived of in my country, and I was strengthened in my gratitude and faith in God. This psychological and spiritual gain urged me to surpass myself when

I returned home. This was particularly true when faced with my neighbors' silence when I asked them who had killed my relatives and where their bodies were. I wanted to give them a decent burial.

Should I let myself be overcome by hatred before my neighbors' indifference? Should I abuse them and threaten them with death? I was not prevented from doing so by any fear of punishment. The values of gratitude and faith that had been instilled in me from an early age and that had healed my wounds during the horror of genocide kept helping me to fight the consequences. Today, these values continue to comfort me. I can but encourage my relatives' killers and all my neighbors to practice them. I am convinced that practicing them will make love prevail over hatred in a self-reconciled society.

CHAPTER 1

MY FATHER, AN ORDINARY CITIZEN

The tactical choice of the Hutu elite ... consisting in overall
denouncing of Tutsi monarchy and even of all the Tutsis
as being responsible for the general suffering of the Hutus
(thereby forgetting the equivalent suffering of Tutsi peasants),
extended this misunderstanding into postcolonial rule.
—Jean-Pierre Chrétien

During Tutsi kingship rule, the majority of the Tutsis led lives similar to those of Hutu peasants. My father belonged to the critically large number of Rwandans who earned their living toiling. He did not belong to any political group. Yet, when it was time to drive out the members of the monarchy nobility and the other Tutsi leaders, my father was among the first Tutsi in the Mugombwa Mission to be listed for death. The only reason for these persecutions was the mention of "Tutsi" in his identity card. But he was also very tall (1.90 meters), a typical feature of the members of this so-called Tutsi ethnic group.

Actually, the Hutus and the Tutsis belong together as Rwandans. They speak the same language and share the same culture, including faith. In Rwanda, there is no specific region for the Hutus or the Tutsis, and since time immemorial they have lived harmoniously together as a community. There is really no ground to identify the Tutsis or the Hutus as members of different ethnic groups. Unfortunately, every Tutsi was marked as an enemy to the nation by the Hutu elite during the so-called 1959 social revolution, and my father was not an exception. All his life, he had to pay for this mistake of being a Tutsi, until he was killed with almost his entire family during the 1994 genocide.

My father's name was Siméon Musabende. He was born in 1934 in Butare, Southern Rwanda, in a place close to the border with Burundi. At that time, Rwanda was ruled by a Tutsi king, the Mwami, who was assisted by chieftains and subchieftains in the administration of the country under Belgian trusteeship. My father was the eldest son in his family and had lost his mother during childhood. His family was Roman Catholic, and he had adopted this choice, as it helped him bear the absence of his mother. He was very devoted to the Virgin Mary, whom he regarded as his own mother. I remember very well that from the time I had the age of reason, he used to gather the whole family at least three times a week in the evening to say the rosary. He loved singing hymns dedicated to the Virgin Mary, especially one about joining her in paradise one day, as Jesus had given her to us for a mother. In addition to this special devotion to the Mother of Jesus, my father used to tell us that daily prayer was a personal habit.

My grandfather was a trading agent for white tradesmen in the town of Butare. In addition to his Kinyarwanda mother tongue, he spoke Kiswahili, a sign of learned person at that time. My father told us that Grandfather wished his son to go to school in order to become an important person. So, when he was six, my father started elementary school, which was located far from his home. He had to walk several kilometers every day.

Besides his commitment to learning, my father also served mass at Gisagara Catholic Mission, and he used to tell us how much he enjoyed it. At that time, there were very few secondary schools, and though he was among the brightest pupils in his class, he was not admitted to secondary school. The Belgian administration was eager to train almost exclusively the sons of great ruling Tutsi families. My father was an ordinary Tutsi and was not lucky enough to proceed beyond the elementary school. Though disappointed, he did not sit idly. He continued to serve mass at Gisagara Catholic Mission.

This steady volunteering at the mission did not go unnoticed by the missionaries. They noted his intelligence and started preparing him to become an elementary school teacher. When he was eighteen, he was already teaching first grade at the neighboring Mugombwa Mission. At twenty, he married my mother, who was eighteen. My mother lost both her parents in early childhood. She had an elder sister, also very young, and they were both raised by their mother's brother. My future mother was also an ardent Catholic, and she never missed Sunday mass.

My father used to tell us that whenever he saw a pretty girl at church on Sunday, he felt a strong urge to make a proposal of marriage. After a short period of dating, he proposed to my mother, and she accepted him. Actually, this pretty girl had also secretly admired the young man for his devotion to prayer. Later on, as a mother, she used to tell us how in her daily prayer she kept asking God for this churchgoer young man to become her husband. He was the kind of man she felt for. Later, Father and Mother used to tell us that from the moment they got acquainted, they were always impatient for the next Sunday, because it was the only day they could afford to meet. At that time, a girl was strictly prohibited from going around alone with a young man. Their only opportunity to talk was after mass on their way back home. My father told us that when he proposed to her she simply replied, "Tell your father to address my family. You know I have no right to answer for myself." My father did as suggested and told his father that he had found the girl of his dreams. As per Rwandan culture, my grandfather had to gather information about my future mother's family.

The first thing to inquire about was whether her family belonged to the Bashingwe clan, which was supposedly associated with ill-fortune in Rwandan traditional society. He also collected information on other taboos likely to prevent the marriage, and fortunately none was found. When the two families finally agreed on everything, my father and my mother were married at Kansi Catholic Mission in the very church where they had first met.

Long before my father's marriage, Grandfather had lost his job, because his employer had gone back to Europe. To earn a living, he turned to raising cattle. Where he lived in Gisagara, grazing land was already scarce, and he decided to move to Mugombwa in a place called Kirarambogo, where my father had already begun teaching first grade in the elementary school.

Together, they started to raise cattle, which developed smoothly, as the pastures were free, good, and plentiful. While my father was teaching, my mother stayed at home managing farm work and supervising the cattle. With raising cattle on top of his teaching job, my father was a respected person in Mugombwa. He used to tell us that with these activities, he could afford to hire workers to help my mother with her housework.

In spite of his success, my father never stopped being a catechist at the mission, something that earned him fame from the mission people and the majority of his neighbors. He used to tell us how during his free time he would go and teach catechism to baptism seekers and how he often happened to be Godfather to many newly baptized Roman Catholics in his mission.

François, the eldest child in our family, was born in 1955. Two years later, my elder sister Bernadette was born. Things had started changing then. Some people from the Hutu ethnic group had started drafting documents on the political direction that they wanted the country to take.

In 1957, Hutu intellectuals led by Grégoire Kayibanda, a former student at a missionary-sponsored seminary, published their *Bahutu Manifesto*. This document called for the emancipation of the Hutus, claiming that Tutsi rule had marginalized them politically. Later, they formed a political party called MDR-PARMEHUTU that started fighting for political change.

In 1959, other political parties were created. In addition to MDR-PARMEHUTU, there were UNAR, a party that supported the king and advocated the unity of the Rwandan people; and APROSOMA, created by Joseph Habyarimana (alias Gitera), a party that rejected kingship and advocated a republican system. My father and my grandfather never associated with any political party. They remained neutral, according to my father.

While monarchy leaders were openly negotiating to obtain the independence of Rwanda, then under Belgian trusteeship, the Hutu leaders took this opportunity to form an alliance with the Belgians in order to remove Tutsi aristocracy. This happened as the Belgians, who had formerly supported Tutsi monarchy, decided to shift their support toward Hutu leaders. The Belgians thought that their new position was justified and argued that from a democratic viewpoint, the Hutus were the majority. But in reality, those Hutu leaders did not represent all Hutus. Some of the Hutus were not against the Tutsi monarchy. This was evidenced by some moderate Hutus who were either exiled or killed during the 1959 revolution.

The support from Belgian authorities was decisive and very encouraging to Hutu leaders who targeted power and the abolishment of the Tutsi monarchy. During this period of tensions, King Mutara III Rudahigwa died in mysterious circumstances toward the end of 1959. Hutu leaders capitalized on this tragic event to abolish the Tutsi monarchy once for all. They organized and won a referendum that sealed their victory, and they politically excluded the parties that supported monarchy. Yet, there was no peaceful change, because Hutu leaders called for hunting down and slaughtering the Tutsis in general, as well as the Hutus who remained faithful to the monarchy.

Hutu leaders' hatred toward the Tutsis was inculcated in public meetings and published in news organs. My father used to tell me about Mr. Joseph, alias Gitera, a Hutu leader living in a neighboring district. This leader dared to publicly proclaim that living with a Tutsi was similar to suffering from stomach cancer or from a sore that would never heal. If the disease was not treated, the victim would eventually die. Therefore, the Tutsis had no alternative other than fleeing or dying. My father's story about Gitera's attitude is confirmed today by various publications on the history of Rwanda.

Even if all of the Hutus were sensitized to fight the Tutsis in general, my parents told me that a considerable number of Hutus were members of the UNAR party, which supported the monarchy and advocated for the unity of the Rwandan people. Nowadays, Rwandans celebrate a National Heroes' Day. One of the heroes is Michel Rwagasana. He was a Hutu and was killed for remaining faithful to the UNAR party and advocating for national unity. Though a cousin to Grégoire Kayibanda, then president of the republic, he was killed together with Tutsi leaders in 1963. His only crime was to side with the Tutsis. Like Rwagasana, some other Hutus did not support the extremist idea of killing the Tutsis.

The next chapter is about the example of two Hutu brothers and their friends who saved my father because they did not share the extremist ideology of exterminating the Tutsis. They acted compassionately and out of love, expecting no reward, and they ran the risk of meeting severe punishment from Hutu extremists. In his belief, my father used to tell me that the two Hutu brothers saved him because they were his brothers in faith. He often repeated this story to me to warn against clichés that all Hutus hated all Tutsis. He also invited me to be faithful to the Christian faith as a sign of recognition to God and to his protectors.

CHAPTER 2

MY FATHER: SAVED BY HIS BROTHERS IN FAITH

The genocide of the Tutsis of Rwanda did not start just a few
hours after the attack of April 6, 1994 but thirty-five years
earlier, very exactly on November 1, 1959. People should know
that from this fateful date, the Tutsis never had any respite in
Rwanda. They were systematically marginalized because of
their alleged ethnic group, and a very small pretext was enough
for them to be killed by thousands or tens of thousands.
—Boris Boubacar Diop

My father told me this: "When I was saved by my Hutu friends, I
took it for a miracle, a true gift from heaven. From that day on, my
attitude has completely changed, and I prayed every day, morning and
evening. I wondered why God had chosen to save me among so many
others." In November 1959, the hunting down and the massacres of
the Tutsis started across the whole of Rwanda. Some Tutsi young
men had beaten up Dominique Mbonyumutwa, a Hutu leader, in
Byimana in the center of the country, which triggered the violence.

From that incident, the propagation of hatred toward the
Tutsis spiraled everywhere in Rwanda; Hutus wanted revenge.

My father remembered that there were placards everywhere with announcements like: "We do not want any more Tutsis in Rwanda; let them go and live elsewhere." Living in the backcountry, my parents first imagined that they would be spared. They were mistaken: the first anti-Tutsi persecutions had started countrywide, and my family was eventually affected.

This period was unforgettable to my father because whenever his life was seriously under threat, he noted that God also performed a miracle. "I was desperate and could not imagine that some Hutus would protect me. Yet, at the last moment, God sent Gérard and Ferdinand to save me from death," he told me. When Hutu extremists started hunting down the Tutsis, setting houses on fire, plundering their property, and cutting down their banana plantations, my father and his entire family left their home, running away from the Hutus who threatened to kill them. They left without knowing where to go.

In my village, my father was the killers' primary target. Since my father was aware of this, he hid in the bush, and the killers decided to go and fetch him from his hiding place. Guessing that he would be uncovered, my father, then only twenty-five years old, ran for his life. As he was running, a group of Hutus behind him shouted that Siméon was to die before all the rest.

When my father saw that they were determined to kill him, he sped up, and they ran after him shouting like hunters after a wild animal. My father told me: "There were so many of them, coming from all sides. They all shouted, and I was desperate; I was lonely, totally left to my fate. Yet, the people after my life were all neighbors of mine, perfectly aware of my innocence." Indeed, my father had committed no offense likely to justify his arrest, but he had to die just because he was a Tutsi.

My father ran with the intention to outrun the killers. Guessing that they would not catch him, the killers called upon other extremists from the nearby localities he was likely to escape through. On his side, my father was very cautious and avoided dangerous routes. At one time, he noted that in addition to the group pursuing him from behind, there was another group in front of him, running and shouting. Uninformed that they were there to save him, he was sure that this group also consisted of Hutus who were after his life. "Both groups were shouting very loudly, the one in front threatening the one behind, and I was at a loss," he told me. Finally, he noted that the group behind him was slowing down while the one in front ran faster. Seeing his end close, he decided to stop running and wait for death. He sat down and started to pray. While he was sitting on the ground, he saw in front of him his teaching mate and friend, Ferdinand, with his brother Gérard. They all came to comfort and sympathize with him. Seeing that the team in front was coming to his rescue and was led by two respected Hutus in the area, the group from behind retreated, totally ashamed. It was my father's first survival but not the end of his persecution.

My father often used to tell me: "The Hutus wanted to kill me, and I was saved by other Hutus." Again, he remained convinced that his faultless friendship with Ferdinand and Gérard was especially based on faith; they were all devout Catholics. They taught other people about God's love, about our creator and father to all. My father also asserted that in this particular case, his protectors had considered affiliation to their Christian family rather than their affiliation to Hutu or Tutsi ethnic groups. He went on saying that though the latter's identities were important in people's lives during that period, the two brothers had chosen to fight their Hutu brotherhood to save their brother in Christ.

Since the day of his first survival, my father noted how vulnerable he was. He told me that it was at that moment that he became convinced that the help of God and other people was more necessary than ever before. Following this, he committed himself with all his heart not to harbor hatred against others. For this reason, whenever I dared abuse these extremist Hutus, he warned me: "Don't behave like people who do not know God. Otherwise, you won't be different from these extremists who do not know God and do not accept him as a father to every man."

After comforting my father, Ferdinand and Gérard left and went to help my mother, brother, and sister, who were still very young. My family found refuge in Ferdinand's home but realizing the imminent danger of attack, they left for the church courtyard at Mugombwa Mission, where they lived for some time. In that place, all the Tutsis driven out of their homes as well as their properties were protected by Belgian soldiers, but they lived under very miserable conditions as my mother used to tell me. After some time at the mission, the local government began to select the Tutsis: some were to leave Rwanda once for all; some others were to be deported to Bugesera region, an inhospitable place, a forest infested with tsetse fly; and a small number of Tutsis who were allowed to go back to their plundered and destroyed homes.

Fortunately, the names of my parents were on the list of those who were allowed to return home and resume their everyday activities in their villages. My father and my grandfather returned to the village, but members of the extended family—my father's uncles, aunts, and their families—left for Burundi and Tanzania. My family's Tutsi friends and neighbors were either killed or obliged to leave the country—some for Burundi, some for Uganda, and others for the Democratic Republic of the Congo.

My father told me about his uncles Sehene and Sefuku and their families, who he would never see again. His cousins Constance and Anastasie, Vénuste, Nsabimana, Iyakaremye and their families were all undesirable in Rwanda and had to leave. Léon Mugesera later regretted expelling the Tutsis from Rwanda. In his speech of November 20, 1992 in Kabaya, seventeen months before the 1994 Tutsi genocide, he said: "We made a big mistake in 1959 to allow you to leave. I was still a child ..." Léon Mugesera was an influential extremist member of the ruling party. He regretted that the Tutsis were allowed to go abroad. Thirty years later, some of them and their children came back in arms to assert their rights.

My father, whose nuclear family had remained almost in isolation, was very anxious but still saw a miracle in all this. He saw an extraordinary sign of heaven and believed that God had saved him to testify his love. For the rest of his life, my father remained grateful for this extraordinary action. Thirty-five years later in 1994, just after the Tutsi genocide, I still remembered this attitude of his. While I was in Italy, I learned that nearly all of my family had been exterminated. It was very painful. But I was also very grateful to God, who had let me out of Rwanda just a few months before the genocide. Since then, I resolved to lead a grateful life even if at the beginning it was difficult, but I progressively became used to it.

From that experience, which he still believed to be a miracle, my father, an ardent Catholic, became even more trusting in God and more churchgoing. He always wondered why he had been allowed to remain in the country while other Tutsis were stripped of their property and driven out of their motherland like animals, simply because they were Tutsis. He viewed returning to his home as a special privilege. He often told us that he had always wondered about the price he had paid to escape the suffering the majority of the Tutsis had experienced. He never forgot these blessings from God.

As said above, my father found his home devastated when he returned. The house was completely destroyed and all his property plundered. He had to start everything from scratch. Only now, many years after the 1994 Tutsi genocide and especially during

12

the commemoration period, does Rwanda Television broadcast the pictures of the 1959 events: the houses on fire, some Tutsis with bound hands and feet, beaten up or killed. All throughout the thirty years of extremist Hutu rule, no documentary of the 1959 events could be broadcast.

My father told us the story of one of his neighbors, Elias. He was a bit honest compared to the other Hutu neighbors. When he saw my father coming back to the village, he found him and returned the things he had looted. This man remained honest and irreproachable even during the 1994 genocide. He did not take part in the killings. Rather, he hid his neighbor Rusaku's children. These children still testify to his courage. Elias protected them in full knowledge that he risked his life. Indeed, Hutu extremists severely punished anyone who dared give shelter to a Tutsi.

When he was with his friends, my father often bitterly told the tragic stories of their friends killed in 1959. He related the particular case of a certain Mutembe, a chieftain of Bashumba-Nyakare. His death was well known in the whole Butare region and probably countrywide. He was tall and big, and the extremists used an axe to kill him.

With these recollections, my father was perfectly aware that injustice would not be over soon. The Tutsis were periodically threatened. Besides, none of the Hutu criminals were ever taken in for questioning or punished. Still more frustrating, after these tragic events, nobody cared and sometimes, the most extremist perpetrators were rewarded and appointed as government officials. Survivors of this period would not dare complain or request justice for fear of being killed.

My father realized that in such a situation, God alone could change something. His total faith, hope, and trust in him showed in his actions as a committed Christian. Though he was an elementary school teacher, he was also known as a good catechist in our mission. His religious commitment was especially a kind of gratitude toward

13

God for his protection, as Father used to assert. This gratitude was also felt and expressed toward the two brothers who had protected him. In Rwandan culture, the most highly valued gift given to a real good friend is a cow. It is in this framework that my father gave Gérard, the first agent of his survival, a heifer to thank him for his loving and courageous act. With this gift, my family and the families of the two brothers became closer and inseparable friends. As said previously, Gérard and Ferdinand had become my father's brothers in Christ.

Coming back to faith in God, traditional Rwandans believed in one God even before the arrival of Western missionaries. All Rwandans, Hutus, or Tutsis believed in *Imana*, God-Protector of Rwanda. They had baptism-like ceremonies, *kubandwa,* where the initiates had Godfathers and Godmothers, just as the Christian religion practices. These ceremonies involved some prohibitions of a moral nature, which were elements of cohesion of Rwandan society. For example, it was an interdiction to harm a religious mate, one who had taken part in the same *kubandwa* ceremony.

European missionaries found out that Rwandans already believed in one God. Faith in *Imana* brought all Rwandans together— the Hutus and the Tutsis. The Rwandans who were converted to Christianity quickly understood that their *Imana* was the same as the Christian God, creator of all men, provider of peace, prosperity and other benefits that are necessary to humanity.

Faith in one God continued to bring Rwandans together, irrespective of their ethnic groups. Even if churches were burned down and many Christians killed their brothers in Christ during the 1994 Tutsi genocide, a few righteous people were noted. A number of survivors were saved by some Hutu Christians who had remained faithful to the end, despite the high risk. Those Hutus were considered traitors by the extremists, but they are now treated as righteous people by all Rwandans.

CHAPTER 3

A SYMBOLIC NAME FOR GRATITUDE TO GOD

The year you were born, 1963, was a more difficult period than
1959. Killings of the Tutsis were widespread and systematic. I
was afraid because I did not see how I could survive once again.
Yet, I did not want to die with a debt and rather than being
overcome by bitterness and despair, I opted for gratitude. For this
reason, I gave you the name of Ndayishimiye, "I thank God."
—My father

In 1963, some Tutsis expelled from Rwanda in 1959 organized in
small groups with little means and attacked Rwanda from exile.
The Hutu extremists inside Rwanda found a good pretext to get rid
of many Tutsis who had remained in the country. Actually, there
had been no respite for the Tutsis since 1959, but the extent of the
1963 Tutsi massacres was unprecedented. It was during this period
that my father feared for his life. Especially at the end of 1963 and
at the beginning of 1964, the Tutsis were systematically killed
in many regions of Rwanda. More particularly, in neighboring
Gikongoro Prefecture, the Tutsis were massively killed irrespective
of age or sex.

The first attacks from Tutsi refugees began in 1961 in the northern region of Byumba Prefecture. In fact, the Tutsis expelled in 1959 had not accepted this humiliation and later sought all means to return to their country. From Uganda, these exiles, nicknamed *Inyenzi* or "cockroaches," attacked the Rwandan districts bordering this country. A number of sources provide unanimous evidence that whenever they attacked, Hutu extremists used those troubled times to make false accusations of complicity against the Tutsis in the country. Actually, Tutsi peasants who lived in the areas attacked by the *Inyenzi* were easily killed without any justice. To escape death, survivors went into exile, giving an opportunity to the assailants to recruit new fighters.

In 1962, small attacks continued in this northern part of Rwanda and were followed by reprisals that always targeted innocent Tutsis. The reprisals continued, and in 1963 the *Inyenzi* attacked the Bugesera area bordering Burundi in the east. The extremist Hutus started killing the Tutsis everywhere in Rwanda, even in areas that were very far from those attacks. It was in those circumstances that the killings started in Gikongoro Prefecture in the south.

My father was informed that the killings would soon reach his village. He also knew that the chance of his survival was now very slim. Compared to 1959, the Tutsis had a very difficult time escaping Rwanda. In 1963, all the borders were protected to stop the attacks but also to stop those who tried to flee.

The tragic and panicky situation coincided with my mother's pregnancy. She was about to deliver. I was born during that fearful period, which changed into happiness because whatever the moment, a new baby is always a source of joy to the family. My father told me that when I was born, the one thing that came to his mind was gratitude toward God, who had kept him alive. The name he gave me at birth was a sign of this heartfelt gratitude.

As a general rule, every name in Kinyarwanda means something. When a baby is born, the parents consult to choose a name that is appropriate to their child. Traditionally, the name was given according to the situation of the family. If the family was having a difficult time or was happy, the name referred to either. Similarly, when the family meant to send a positive or negative message to their acquaintances, the child would bear the name with this message. When parents wished their child to use a well-known, brave person as a model, the baby was given the name of that person. And when they wanted to express how desperate they were in a given situation or how grateful they were toward someone, the baby's name expressed their state of mind.

It is in this framework that at birth, I was given by Father the name of Ndayishimiye, or "I thank God." With my name, my father told me that he wanted to thank God for everything he had done for him, especially in the very difficult moments mentioned above: "Your birth was a special occasion to solemnly thank God for all the protection he had given my family since 1959. But as I had no hope to survive in 1963, I also wanted to leave a durable heritage with you and all my children. A heritage which could not be plundered, burned, or destroyed in any other way."

For my father, the duty of gratitude prevailed over panic and despair caused by the killings of the Tutsis. He knew that in 1959 God had protected him in the last minute through the two brothers. He told me that he had to concentrate on the positive element in the middle of so much confusion by giving me a name of gratitude. My father insisted that this attitude made him strong enough to go on living somewhat normally and to face the threats coming from all the corners of the country. My father gave me the heritage of seeking the positive in very difficult situations and thanking the author of this kindness. So far, this heritage has been a driving force for everything I undertake in my life.

The 1963 Tutsi killings and those in the early months of 1964 shocked some expatriates who were living in Rwanda. It was in this framework that some of them informed the international community. Globally, there were very few condemnations of those killings, but the Vatican Radio already qualified them as genocide. Better still, Bertrand Russell, a mathematician, philosopher, and Nobel Prize winner for literature in 1950, qualified the killings as "the most horrible and systematic massacres of human beings ever seen since the extermination of the Jews by the Nazis."[1]

Considering that the killings were a blatant scandal, President Kayibanda sent emissaries to Europe to explain what had happened, laying special emphasis on the fact that Rwanda had been attacked. However, thanks to those denunciations, President Kayibanda stopped the killings, but many Tutsis had perished in the meantime. Some sources estimated between eight and ten thousand Tutsis were killed in Gikongoro Prefecture alone.

No Rwandan dared denounce the massacres publicly. It should be remembered that the leaders of the opposition parties, like UNAR and RADER, had just been killed. Michel Rwagasana and Joseph Rutsindintwarane were among them. They perished under horrible conditions in Ruhengeri Prison. By killing those opposition leaders, the Kayibanda government intimidated and hence dissuaded all those who could denounce the horrors by eliminating all opposition parties. All those dead remained unaccounted for, and no one was held responsible for those killings. The Tutsi survivors of the massacres were humiliated and made submissive; they had no one to speak for them. The ruling MDR-PARMEHUTU was the only remaining political party in Rwanda, thus the extremists were left to enjoy total impunity.

---

[1] Boris Boubacar Diop, « le [Document exclusif] Génocide des Tutsi du Rwanda: un juge français contre un autre : et les africains dans tout ca ?», www.thiesvision.com, 31 janvier 2012.

Luckily enough, my father was saved for the second time, along with his whole family, and he saw this as a new miracle. Besides verbal threats, my father was not harmed in any other way during that period. He considered his survival a great favor, a privilege that many Tutsis did not obtain. As far back as I can remember, I listened to my father's tragic stories but also to the wonders God had performed for him. He used to recall them in the evening when all the family gathered after the evening meal. At that time, we had no electrical power. Instead, we were using a hurricane lamp for light. I remember perfectly well that my father always concluded these stories with a prayer before we went to bed.

My father's grateful inclination was so strong that my four younger brothers and my sister all had names referring to God. Antoine was born in 1965 and had a name of hope, *Uyizeye*, or "One who trusts God." Marthe, my younger sister was born in 1967 and given the name of *Uwanyiligira*, or "a gift to God." Emile, born in 1969, had the name of *Hitayezu*, or "Jesus is the one who gives a name."

Godefroid was born in 1973, another difficult period for the Tutsis, and my father gave him the name of *Twagirumukiza*, or "only Jesus can save us." The youngest in the family was born in 1976 and was given the name of *Bayisenge*, or "let them pray to God." This name referred to my father's friends who still practiced *kubandwa* and *kuraguza* ceremonies, Rwandan religious rituals, especially widespread before the advent of Christianity. Christians called these traditional practices heathen and treated them as such. With this name, my father invited his friends to pray to God rather than go and seek solutions with the wizards.

My parents considered our names as gifts, not of money or any other material form but from the spirit, free of hatred. "Hatred is very contagious and dangerous, and I do not want any of my children to grow with this anti-value," my father declared. He was convinced that practicing gratitude toward God and having faith and hope in him was the best way to survive in Rwanda, which killed the Tutsis whenever and however it wished.

Because of this piety, my family sometimes experienced strong pressure from some of our friends who often invited us to take part in *kuraguza*, or divination, and other practices involved in traditional religion. Those practices were prohibited by the Catholic Church. Before being baptized in the Catholic Church, the new believers had to vow to give up these other practiced. Families discovered by the Catholic authority to indulge in these practices were no longer authorized to receive the sacraments in the Church until they were reintegrated. But in spite of everything, some Rwandans never gave up their traditional religion while also practicing in the Catholic Church.

My family had definitely given up the traditional religion for the Christian faith, and our friends and neighbors knew it. The family was cited among the best Catholic Christian families in Mugombwa parish. The living evidence was that my father and my mother became Godfather and Godmother to many new believers in our parish. Even my father's two protectors chose my parents for their children. My mother was Godmother to Colette, Ferdinand's daughter, while my father was Godfather to Juvénal, Gérard's son. The other Hutu and Tutsi families followed suit. Joseph chose my mother as Godmother to her daughter Anisia, and Berthe chose my father as Godfather to his son Jean-Bosco. This bond between Christian Tutsis and Hutus promoted deep friendship between members of their families.

My family shared consistent faith in God with some other Tutsis who had survived the 1963 massacres. My friend, the priest Jérôme Masinzo, was also born in 1963 in Gikongoro Prefecture. He told me that his whole family took refuge in the Kaduha Parish church after the extremists drove them out of their home, which was subsequently destroyed. When the killings were over, his father decided to build a new house quite close to the church, planning to take refuge there when the persecutions of the Tutsis resumed.

When he was old enough to choose his profession, Jérôme became a priest in the Catholic Church. During the 1994 genocide, he was a parish priest at Ngoma, in the Butare Diocese, and he hid there until the end of the horrendous events. He suffered so much and survived by a hair's breadth. Almost all of his family was decimated. In 1990, Jérôme's family had experienced another tragedy. His sister was a secondary school student in Gisenyi and was killed after being tortured, supposedly to avenge the Hutu soldiers who were being killed on the front trying to repel the attack of the Rwandan Patriotic Front, mostly Tutsis.

In spite of his unfortunate story, Jérôme is not hateful today. Rather, he helped women in Karama Parish to create an association called *Ubutwari bwo kubaho,* or "Be courageous and survive." This association brings together Tutsi women widowed by the genocide and women whose husbands are in jail as genocide perpetrators. This group of women is a touching example of unity and reconciliation in Rwanda.

Even if gratitude and faith in God were a priority in hard times for some Tutsis, other Tutsis were desperate and referred to their misfortune when choosing names for their children. For example, a girl and classmate my age was called *Nyiramakuba,* "misfortune bearer." In Buvumo, a small locality in the former Bashumba Nyakare province, a certain Kigenza gave his son, born in 1961, the name of *Nyamaswa,* "the animal." This father wanted to express his desolation by saying that his son was like an unfortunate animal born on a hunting day.

I was acquainted with Nyamaswa when he was an adolescent. He had lost his father and his uncle Mutembe (killed with an axe) when he was still a baby. Nyamaswa "the animal" lived with his mother, sister, and two brothers. Fortunately, women and children were not yet targeted at that time. Such names as "Nyamaswa" evoked not only the events of the time but also the events to come, like those of 1994.

Nyamaswa and Nyiramakuba's families were exterminated during the 1994 genocide. There were many other children who also bore names that referred to that period. Védaste, a friend of mine, was left the only survivor in his family. His father had given him the name of Mbarubukeye, "I do not know if I'll be alive tomorrow." I know a man called Baranyanga, "they hate me." Names referring to these hard times are many and leave a historical mark of the state of mind of a category of Rwandans at that time.

It is a possibility that many Rwandans do not know or remember the 1963 and 1964 events. Where I am concerned, I cannot forget my knowledge that the anti-Tutsi killings of my birth year and the year that followed were first to be qualified as genocide. I cannot forget either that many testimonies have emphasized the cruelty of those killings. But my father's attitude taught me that gratitude toward God must be practiced in happy as well as in hard times if we want to go forward in life.

CHAPTER 4

MY AWARENESS OF THE DANGER OF BEING A TUTSI

Rwandan youth, in a spontaneous revolutionary movement,
have reminded the authorities that they would not tolerate
the weakness or abuse of power tending to betray the 1959
Popular Revolution and to cheat the people of its conquests.
—A motion by Rwandan Hutu students in Belgium on the
socioethnic problem in Rwanda. March 10, 1973.

My parents often told me about the 1959 popular revolution, when many Tutsis went into exile for the first time. They also evoked the killings of many Tutsis in 1963–1964, and I couldn't believe these events could happen again. The 1973 threats and killings were especially attributed to the revolutionary youth, as the 1994 genocide was attributed to the so-called popular anger following the death of the president!

But the 1973 hunting down of Tutsi civil servants and students could hardly be the initiative of only the revolutionary youth. For this period, as for the previous ones, the perpetrators of crimes have justified the events in their own way. There were no opposition political parties, because they had been abolished when most of their leaders were killed, as said in the previous chapter. There were no independent and human rights associations—no press or justice. Those persecutions against the Tutsis remained unaccounted for, totally anonymous.

I was ten years old then, in fourth grade. I saw everything, attentive to each event. At the beginning of the 1973 persecutions, I saw my cousin Thaddée, a student at Groupe Scolaire de Butare, return home totally devastated. He had been sent away, together with the other Tutsis at that prestigious school. Thaddée told us how their Hutu classmates drove them out brutally: "A group of Hutu students fell on us during the night, holding clubs and iron bars, and striking every Tutsi at hand. There were many wounded, and we spent the night in the bush before returning to our families."

All Tutsi students were driven out of their schools everywhere in Rwanda. My father was afraid and sought information everywhere. When he came back in the evening, he would inform us of what was happening everywhere, in the town of Butare and elsewhere in the country: "All Tutsi professors and students at the National University of Rwanda and teachers at secondary and primary schools in Butare Town were beaten up and forcibly sent away. All civil servants in this town met the same plight." In the prefectures of Gikongoro and Gitarama, neighboring the prefecture of Butare, the extremist Hutus had already started killing people. With Father's information, we all panicked and felt ourselves to be easy targets. To comfort us, he called us to prayer.

Our parents told us that in 1961, 1963, 1964, and 1966, Hutu extremists drove out and killed the Tutsis in Rwanda, supposedly because Tutsi refugees had attacked the country from abroad. Curiously enough, there was no refugee attack in 1973. Evidence showed that refugee attacks had stopped in 1967. The only reason for the 1973 persecutions of the Tutsis who had remained in Rwanda was that there were too many of them in schools and public service, at least according to the extremist viewpoint.

In February 1973, my classmates, children like myself, told me that all the Tutsis were going to be killed. I noted that those children were well informed, and many were vicious and impatient. My Hutu classmates' favorite conversation during the break was about violence against the Tutsis taking place in the other regions of Rwanda. They took advantage of breaks to harass us, saying that killings were going to start very soon in our own district.

Our administrative sector was situated in a mountainous area along Akanyaru River, between Rwanda and Burundi. It was a kind of backcountry; the only important people were elementary school teachers. With the hunting down of the Tutsis, these were also the Hutus' first targets. But living in the backcountry was a relative advantage when compared to the Tutsis living in towns. Actually, the killings reached the backcountry when the operation was over in towns. Our geographical position at the border was somehow a great advantage in times of persecution. Between the Akanyaru River and the mountains, there was a large valley covered with very dense papyrus that was used as a hiding place for Tutsis in times of trouble.

This papyrus was a kind of protection and saved many Tutsis. However, those who were discovered were drowned in this river right away. Fishermen who were friends to our family used to tell us horrible stories of the bodies they passed floating on Akanyaru River in those mad times. In 1973, there was no television in Rwanda, and international reporters were nowhere to be found to report on events in my country. Actually, I got a full understanding of the fishermen's stories during the 1994 Tutsi genocide. Pictures of bodies floating in Akanyaru River and Lake Victoria were shown during the first weeks of genocide commemoration. Today, those images stick in my memory and bring back the fishermen's tales as well as other tales about the Tutsis who were thrown into the Mwogo, Mbirurume, and Rukarara rivers in Gikongoro Prefecture in 1963–1964.

Coming back to the events at our elementary school, Thomas, a schoolboy in fifth grade loved saying: "When the killings start, we will start with Siméon's family for sure." My family was always taken by our neighbors as pure Tutsis. They referred to our size because we were all very tall. The most distinctive Tutsi feature was height, and we were targeted before the rest. Moreover, my father and grandfather had herds of cattle, an activity also considered typical to the Tutsis, even if some Hutus also practiced it.

As Father often reminded me of how I was to behave in front of the threats from my classmates, he also evoked the meaning of my name: "Remember, I gave you the name of Ndayishimiye, and be sure, God is with us." With these words, I was curious to know the meaning of my classmates' names. Surprisingly enough, Paul, son to Ferdinand, the Hutu who had saved my father in 1959, had the name of *Habinshuti* or, "friends exist." I did not know why he was given this name by his parents, but it evoked the importance of friendship. Another classmate's name was *Kazihise*, or "born after the rain." Here again, I was unable to understand the meaning behind his parents' choice, but they probably referred to rain as violence.

Curiously, there was also a boy whose name was *Mpitabakana*, "when I pass by, they are grinding their teeth." He had a brother with the name of *Banyangiriki*, "why do they hate me?" Unfortunately, Mpitabakana was part of the group of militiamen who killed my parents in 1994. He confessed before the popular courts that were set up to prosecute the genocide perpetrators in Rwanda. For me, a believer in the transmission of hatred or love from parents to children, I have no doubt that Mpitabakana inherited this hatred, which determined his involvement as a genocidaire.

26

The poor child already bore a name of hatred. In 1973, when he was ten, he saw his entourage driving out or killing the Tutsis in impunity, and he was certainly convinced that the Tutsis were the kind of enemy that had to be killed. His active participation in the 1994 genocide is a kind of evidence of this. He was arrested and jailed. He was detained for a few years, and then he confessed and was released after a period of involvement in community reparation work intended to be a probationary period before definitive release. Today, I have no doubt that Mpitabakana was a victim of the education he had received.

In her confession before the Nyamirambo popular courts, journalist Valérie Bemeriki confirmed the idea of transmission of hatred against the Tutsis from Hutu adults to their children: "I am sorry for all the innocent victims. When I was still young, I was always taught that the Tutsis were evil ... Then, the message I was to broadcast when I became a journalist was clear: complete the 1959 revolution ... The Tutsis are evil and must be killed ... I understood that my duty was to get rid of the enemy with the only weapon availed to me, the microphone."[2]

Other children threatened me, but the news that made me panicky concerned the killings of the Tutsi in Gitarama and other areas in Rwanda. I also saw Tutsi civil servants turned out of their jobs fleeing to Burundi. My uncle Alfred who was teaching at a secondary school in Nyanza was forced out, along with his family, and we came to learn that he had been arrested at Nyabitare trading center, when he was trying to flee to Burundi.

We learned that our Hutu neighbors had prevented him from fleeing, had taken all his money and beaten him up. He was unable to proceed toward Burundi or to return home. Alfred, his wife, and

---

[2] www.hirondellenews.com, « 07.12.09-Rwanda/Gacaca-Repentir d'une ancienne journaliste de la RTLM », 7 décembre 2009.

children were at the mercy of extremists. Some days later, with the intervention of Father Claude Simard, he was released with the provision that he stay with his parents in the neighboring district of Muganza.

My father was frightened but went to work as usual. However, he had started to gather information on ways to take us to Burundi. I remember very well that in his daily prayers, he would add special prayers for the situation. He used to tell us: "My children, pray constantly in these hard times. More specifically, ask God to convert these extremists for them to stop persecuting the innocent, and, please, abstain from hating anyone."

One day, he caught me saying that the Hutus were very evil and deserved death also. He told me: "Don't abuse the Hutus, because some of them saved my life. Paul, your number one friend is a Hutu. How dare you say they are all evil and deserve death? How can we pray while nurturing hatred? Well, if you want God to listen to our prayers and to save you, stop hatred; rather, ask God to save us as he has always done." After those pieces of advice, I felt a positive change in me, and I was convinced that he was telling the truth.

Quite often, Grandfather came to ask Father how they were going to flee. One day, when they had finished planning their escape, Joseph came around. He was a respected Hutu and official of MDR-PARMEHUTU at the grassroots level. He was also a friend to my father, who had given him a cow. He was riding a motorcycle, and when Grandfather heard the noise of the engine, he came quickly to listen to Joseph's advice.

The discussion between Joseph, Father, and Grandfather resulted in our family's decision not to flee until Joseph gave us a sign to leave. Father and Grandfather were relieved. Joseph went back home, and we were left without worry. Seeing an official of the ruling party in the region had paid us a visit, the extremist Hutus who were ready to launch an attack on us postponed it.

During the evening prayer, Father invited us to thank God, who had sent Joseph to prevent us from fleeing without knowing where to go. Besides being a respected political personality, Joseph was a school inspector in Ndora-Nyaruhengeri Sector, close to ours. He was also a friend to the school inspector of Kibayi-Muganza Sector where my father was teaching. This made Father more confident concerning his work.

Thanks to Joseph's visit, I went to school a courageous and mentally strong boy the next day. Before the visit, I did not understand how we could leave for Burundi and live in refugee camps with so many problems. This moral strength did not last, however. During the break, a classmate called Charles who always harassed me found me with a group of schoolboys and told me: "All the Tutsis in Kirarambogo will be killed, starting with your family." I was desperate, and my moral strength collapsed. When I got home, I told Father what Charles had said. Father calmed me down saying: "Don't mind; Charles knows nothing on this subject. It's a child's talk." Yet, I saw grief in his eyes in spite of his trying to hide it.

Meanwhile, it was time for the radio news. My father rushed to listen. Afterward, he was unable to hide the grief. He said that on the whole the news warned the Tutsis, telling them to leave in time. In Kinyarwanda, the phrase is *agapfa kaburiwe ni impongo,* or "an antelope shall die in spite of the warning," or "You are forewarned. Don't wait for death to come to you." The evening news closed with this Rwandan proverb. We panicked, and nobody knew what was to be done. Father and Mother called us to prayer. I noted that Father was discouraged but was trying to hide it. After prayer, we went to bed, uncertain and worried.

As usual, my parents went to work the next day, and the children to school. During the break, Charles harassed me once again: "Did you listen to the radio? You leave, or you shall be killed." It was devastating. On top of harassment at school came the daily bad evening news from the radio, as well as news about many Tutsis from other regions in Rwanda leaving for Burundi. Fortunately, Paul was always around. He invited me to play. He tried to help me forget the bad situation. Paul has not changed and lives in the same village. Concerning Charles, nobody knows where he is.

Father's Tutsi friends often gathered in our house to discuss the alternative between fleeing and staying in Rwanda. They came especially for two reasons: Father had good information since he was the friend of an important Hutu, Joseph. Second, he had a lot of banana plantations managed by Mother, and we often had *urwagwa*, a high-quality banana wine brewed by my mother. She produced a large quantity, sold some, and kept the rest at home for our visitors, especially Father's teacher friends. They spent nights discussing their frustrations and humiliation.

In the conversation, Father and his friends often cited and counted the names of the Tutsis killed during that period and all the previous attacks. Eventually, they would note the high number of the dead and say it would be their turn, since there was no sign of an end to the persecutions. They were unable to make a decision between leaving and not leaving. Marc from Muganza and Antoine from Cyumba sadly enumerated the names of their former classmates who had been killed nationwide. They had information on every prefecture and would conclude saying that there was no future for the Tutsis in Rwanda.

Every time Father finished discussing with his friends, I asked him questions. Seeing my concern, he always tried to minimize the problem and give me hope: "Don't mind. This situation won't last. I gave you the name of Ndayishimiye to give you a permanent reminder that God had saved me and would go on protecting us. Don't worry; life will come back to normal very soon." I am unable to express the soothing value of Father's words about God keeping his protection on us! Before going to bed, he would gather us to thank God for keeping us alive while some other Tutsis were being humiliated, killed, or exiled.

The news was increasingly bad each day. Father told us stories about other Tutsi civil servants losing their jobs, traders being jailed, and other Tutsis being killed or fleeing. In the confusion, Father would go and seek advice from Father Claude Simard, our parish priest. The priest always asked him to keep quiet, pray constantly, and, more specifically, to stay where he was and not go abroad. Joseph would visit us every two days. Anyway, in spite of the threats, my family was comforted by friends, unlike many other Tutsis.

Despite his friends' advice, my father decided one day to flee, because the verbal threats of some Hutus were beyond bearing. Fortunately, he went to say good-bye to Father Simard before leaving. To show Father he had to stay, the priest went and found the Hutus making threats and had them change their minds. Father Simard was respected thanks to his development activity that created jobs for many people at Kirarambogo. Eventually, convinced we would not be killed, my family stayed in Rwanda with Father Simard's intervention. Father believed he had been sent by God.

Father Simard was a Canadian missionary and a senior priest at our small Kirarambogo parish. Before his arrival, Kirarambogo was part of the more important Mugombwa Parish. Father Simard was unable to speak our Kinyarwanda language properly, and it was very funny to listen to him. But I loved listening to his teaching during mass. Quite often in his sermons, he would tell us how we all had one father, God our creator. And his recommendation was to love one another as the children of one father if we wanted to please God. He would joke: "Though I am white, I have the same father as you. And if you go on messing things about, you will not be my brothers, and God will not be your father." In fear of losing this precious relationship with my much admired star, I tried to be perfect in everything I did.

Father Simard was loved by the population of Kirarambogo in general, even by non-Catholics. He was the first white man to settle in that area, which was regarded as backward. Before his arrival, there was no sign of economic development. Even the elementary school classrooms were insufficient. For many, classes were held in the shadow of a tree. Father Simard came and built good classrooms from weather-resistant materials.

Before he came to Kirarambogo, the nearest health center was in Gisagara, twenty kilometers away. To solve the problem, he built a health center and brought white nurses to care for the whole population of Kirarambogo and the neighboring areas. Later, he brought drinking water and trained people how to grow rice for the first time in the Akanyaru River Valley. His training and achievements in development fetched respect from many Rwandans. Along these lines, he received a medal from the president of the Republic in 1987. Father, as a collaborator and friend to Father Simard, was very proud of his achievements and capitalized on the advantages related to this friendship.

Support from an important person like Father Simard was essential for my father, and he was very grateful to him. Gratitude toward God was a constant sentiment with him. In my family, daily morning and evening prayer and churchgoing on every Sunday were regular practices. My father used to sing, expressing his gratitude this way, especially through psalms and hymns to the Virgin Mary.

One day his friend Marc surprised him singing and asked why he was singing so loudly, all by himself. Father told him that he could not help it whenever he remembered what God had done for him in his life. After such an unusual answer, Marc, who had asked the question just for a joke, was really affected. Father then built on this to tell him the love story between God and our family. I remember this conversation between the two men very well because before it came to an end, Father saw me and called me. I went to him and he told Marc: "My son's name is Ndayishimiye. I must always be grateful to God for his intervention during my moments of persecution."

My father's tendency to entrust himself unto God in hard times was shared by other people. Emmanuel, a friend of mine, was born in 1973. He told me that when he was born, his father was a prisoner for the offense of being a Tutsi. When he learned that his wife had had a baby boy, he supplicated his district prison authorities for a short leave to go and name his newborn son.

Surprisingly, the district burgomaster not only gave the leave but also released him. But before releasing him, he exacted one condition: "You must constantly wear a medallion bearing President Kayibanda's photograph." He willingly accepted the condition. He had already prepared his son's name when he got home. He gave him the name of *Ndagijimana*, "I entrust him unto God." Thanks to the baby, he had just been released. For him, there was no doubt about God's hand in all this. He was ever grateful to God but also kept wearing the medal with President Kayibanda's picture.

In July of that year, Major General Juvénal Habyarimana successfully made a putsch and overthrew Grégoire Kayibanda. Despite this change, Emmanuel's father forgot to remove the medallion of the deposed president. One day, an official of the new ruling party learned about a man wearing the former president's medallion; he arrested and immediately jailed him. A few months of detention later, he was released. As Emmanuel testified, his father always declared that Tutsi survival was in the hands of God. Through the name he had given his son, he was sure that only God would protect him.

Major General Juvénal Habyarimana came from Gisenyi in northern Rwanda. At school, we were taught that the putsch was a reaction against regionalism promoted by the Kayibanda government. These northern Hutus accused Kayibanda of giving privileges to people from Gitarama, his own birth region, and of marginalizing people from the other regions. With the new government, President Habyarimana stopped the massacres of the Tutsis for a time, but the humiliations and discrimination at work, school, or in the universities continued.

At elementary school, every schoolchild had a serial card detailing personal information, including designation of ethnic group. This card was used to segregate, since access to secondary school was based on a quota system: only 10 percent of spaces were allocated to Tutsis. Students were not selected according to their performance at exams but according to the government-imposed system. The Tutsis were aware that the possibility of furthering their studies beyond elementary school was only a matter of luck.[3]

Ethnic control was normal at elementary schools during that period. Each year, all school teachers had to submit a report detailing the number of Hutu and Tutsi schoolchildren in their classes. We were made to stand up in groups according to our ethnic group. When a schoolchild happened to ignore where he/she belonged, the teacher asked for the father's name, and this information helped to rule out any mistake. I remember well: a teacher once asked me what my ethnic group was, and I kept silent because I was perfectly aware that he knew who I was. Eventually he said: "Oh! You are Siméon's son. Therefore, you are a Tutsi."

---

[3] The educational system in Rwanda consists of four levels: nursery school, elementary school (six years), secondary school (six years), and university or equivalent programs. Secondary school is divided into two parts: the first three years or middle school (general program) and the last three years or high school (majoring program).

After elementary school, I was aware that my chances to go to secondary school were very slim. My good performance at the end of elementary school was useless. Indeed, I was not admitted to secondary school. On paper, the Tutsis had 10 percent of the available places, but in practice, they had even less. In sixth grade, I was second in a class of forty. Perpétue was first, but unfortunately, she was also a Tutsi like myself and was not lucky enough to be admitted to secondary school. Failing admission to secondary school was very hard for me. It all came to mean that I was condemned, as private secondary schools were scarce and very expensive.

Another opportunity to go to secondary school was to successfully sit for an admission exam at a minor seminary. To be admitted there, a written exam was necessary, but other criteria were also considered. First of all, there was a preselection for those who would be admitted to take the exam. I had no problem at this stage: I was an ardent Catholic and was even a member of the parish choir. Better still, I had good grades at the end of elementary school. I sat for the exam, and the outcome was good. I was on the list of those who had passed it. Unfortunately, another list was produced later, and my name had been removed. I was completely disappointed and realized my chances to go to secondary school were over. Minor seminaries in Rwanda were good schools, providing good scientific training as well as humanities education. Because of this, parents who could afford it sought placement for their children, not because they should be trained to become priests but just for a good education. Sometimes, admission to a minor seminary was also a matter of luck rather than performance.

During this selection period for the minor seminary, our parish priest, Father Simard, was in Canada. When he came back, he was disappointed that I had not been admitted. But in our discussion, he eventually assured me that there were other possibilities, if I really meant to be a priest. In the meantime, looking forward for another alternative to secondary school, I registered at a private school for technical training in construction for three years.

When I finished this training, Father Simard hired me in his carpentry workshop at Kirarambogo. His intention was to see if I really had a calling for priesthood. A year later, he told me: "You made it. The test was successfully passed, because in addition to being a model at work, you have been regular in the parish choir. Now start meditating and choosing which religious family you would like to join."

CHAPTER 5

SEARCHING FOR
ANOTHER IDENTITY

We too, Your Lordships, are against caste-based privileges, against
injustice, and we support Human Rights. But in our opinion when you
go as far as saying that one race may not dominate another race, you
should also be courageous enough to say who is dominating who in
Rwandan present context. Tell us, Your Lordships, why is your clergy
mostly Tutsis? ... Do the Tutsis have a particular Catholic calling?
—A motion from Rwandan Hutu students in Belgium on
the socioethnic issue in Rwanda. March 10, 1973.

The Rwandan people were accustomed to the quota system that had
been established to prevent Tutsis from accessing free education and
employment. But the application of this system to prevent the Tutsis
from choosing religious life was beyond understanding. According to
these Hutu elites studying in Belgium, there were more Tutsi than Hutu
priests in Rwanda. According to their philosophy, this was not normal.
These students would be future ministers and senior executives in their
own country. Even if officially Hutu students in Belgium had made
their opinion public, this kind of criticism against the Church was
already familiar in politics in the government of Grégoire Kayibanda.

When Major General Juvénal Habyarimana came to power, some Tutsis dared to hope for some positive change concerning their fundamental rights. However, the Second Republic initiated no change at all. Rather, discrimination was reinforced in all sectors of life. In 1975, two years after the putsch, Habyarimana created a political party called MRND (National Revolution Movement for Development). This party reigned supreme, having no opposition parties, and all Rwandans had to be members. They were even obliged to indulge in what was called "political animation," a kind of singing, dancing, and praise-making used for the exaltation of the ruling party and its founder. Habyarimana was given the title of *Umubyeyi w'igihugu*, "the father of the nation." Unfortunately, he practiced discrimination against part of the population.

As it is often very difficult to differentiate between Hutus and Tutsis, the identity card was very instrumental. At eighteen, every Rwandan citizen had to go to the local government office to get one, with the designation of one of the ethnic groups: Hutu, Tutsi, or Twa. For example, the administration had to fill my identity card with reference to my father's. His card bore his designation as a Tutsi. Therefore, I was a Tutsi, and this had to appear on my identity card.

The card was used as a discriminatory tool par excellence against the Tutsis, but ethnic groups in the proper sense did not really exist in Rwanda. The card created an illusion of identity to help better enforce discrimination. The value and weight given to ethnic designation was very important. This is the reason why some Tutsis, in order to enjoy privileges reserved for Hutus, tried to falsify their cards. But there were regular checks, and offenders were fined.

Only very few Tutsis have successfully cheated this way. A friend of my father's had a Hutu mother and a Tutsi father, and he tried to obtain a Hutu identity card. Actually, he hoped the local administration authorities would consider his mother's ethnic group.

He had also married a Hutu woman with the aim of changing his identity card. With his mother's family's help, he obtained the much-desired card. Later, the local authorities found out he had changed his card illegally. For punishment, he had to pay a lot of money, and his Tutsi card was returned to him. The poor guy was frustrated and indebted for a long time.

Discrimination against the Tutsis in Rwanda was not limited to state areas of activity but was also widespread in the Church. It was common knowledge that the Kayibanda government had started requesting leaders of the local church to limit the number of the Tutsis in their institutions. Following in their footsteps, the Habyarimana government recommended the application of the quota system to church leaders to achieve ethnic balance. According to the information that I was able to gather, those recommendations were from time to time implemented by some church authorities. It was not surprising, since the Archbishop of Kigali, Vincent Nsengiyumva, was a member of the central committee of the ruling party. Sometimes, problems were reported among Hutu and Tutsi priests when one of them was to be appointed a church authority. The best known example is the case of Félicien Muvara. He was officially appointed second bishop in the Diocese of Butare and was forced to resign even before he was consecrated, all because he was a Tutsi.

In spite of their persecution of Tutsis, Hutu extremists did not manage to prevent them from going into the religious world. Minor and major seminaries continued to welcome a good number of them, especially because young Hutus were attracted by the privileges reserved for them by the government. Most of my Tutsi acquaintances who had been to secondary school or another form of higher education had done so in religious institutions and seminaries. From these, they would obtain good training, and some would become priests in the local church or members of international congregations. Others would quit the religious world and seek jobs in public or private institutions.

As schools training for priesthood were the only educational opportunities Tutsis could secure without discrimination, the majority of Rwandan priests were Tutsis. In Mugombwa Parish, where I belonged before the creation of the small Kirarambogo Parish, all the priests and candidates to priesthood were Tutsis. Mathieu Ngirumpatse was the first priest from Mugombwa; Jean-Bosco Yirirwahandi was next; and Callixte Uwitonze was third. Vital Rutayire and Wellars Mugengana also Tutsis were then in the terminal years of the major seminary. It was cases like these that irritated the Hutu extremists who verbally attacked the bishops to bring them to reduce the number of the Tutsis in seminaries.

Having observed that even bishops were an object of criticism from the Hutu elite, supposedly for hosting many Tutsis in their institutions, my father told me: "Since you want to be a priest, choose an international religious community, and when the extremist Hutus are after us again, I am sure you will be evacuated by those foreign religious people." My father was used to seeing Tutsi persecutions and was aware of the importance of belonging to an international religious community. He told me that the extremists were afraid of white people, and that whenever the Tutsis were under threat, those under the protection of their religious communities had fewer problems. I totally agreed with him on the subject, knowing the international religious communities were composed of people from different races and countries.

I had all the information concerning admission to an international religious community. I had talked with Father Simard about it. He had previously helped and supported my elder brother Alexandre, who was already in the Brothers of Saint Gabriel community. My brother's example invited me to step into his shoes. He used to come back to our family in the village for visits, often along with fellow Western brothers. They came in their car, something rather rare in our village. At that time, only two people had cars in our whole parish: Father Simard and Monique, a Belgian woman in charge of the health center. Our neighbors, seeing Alexandre arrive in their community car, believed he was an important person. However, he was only an ordinary teacher at his community's center for the deaf-mute.

Concerning his studies, Alexandre had been able to proceed, thanks to this community. After elementary school, he had been lucky enough to be admitted at a good public school, the Groupe Scolaire Officiel de Butare. But his luck was short-lived. After three years of middle school, he was denied high school, all in spite of his good grades. The only way left to continue was through seminary. After a short period of religious life, the government admitted him at the same school that had previously refused him, and he graduated. Shortly later, he went to a university in France, where he graduated with a master's degree in Psychology. Presently, he is the director of a secondary school in Rwanda. Many other young Tutsis had been able to become educated, thanks to religious life.

In our school center, many other Tutsi schoolchildren had not been admitted to public secondary school just because they were Tutsis. The best known such case was Alphonse Rugambwa. He was a gifted schoolboy, always ranking first in his class; but his name was not found on the list of successful candidates to secondary school. Later, he joined a religious community, was admitted to secondary school in Bukavu, the Democratic Republic of the Congo, and completed it. After a period as a novice in Cyangugu at the Jesuits,' he was admitted to various universities and finally graduated at the famous university of La Sorbonne in France.

What I liked in religious communities, which I was acquainted with at that time, was the multiracial character of their members. In

Rwanda, my brother Alexandre lived with Frenchmen, Canadians, Hutus, and Tutsis. He spent two years in the Congo Brazzaville as a novice, living with Congolese, Central Africans, and Gabonese. He never saw any discrimination. Like the Brothers of Saint Gabriel, the other religious communities had members from different countries. Some of these communities include the Salesians, the Brothers of Christian Schools, the Brothers of Charity, etc. All of these communities had branches in various countries, and this gave their members an international family. Such diversity in unity made a good impression upon me and pricked my curiosity.

Following my brother's example at the Brothers of Saint Gabriel and Alphonse's at the Jesuits,' I finally decided to take my step. But I still had to make my choice and apply to a specific community. I went to Father Simard for advice. When he saw my grades, he was surprised that I had not been admitted to a public school. I confirmed that I wanted to be a priest, and he connected me with the Rogationists living in Mugombwa.

The community included Father Arturo. He was always a happy guy, good to everybody. There were also Father Giorgio, always quiet and kind; Father Tiziano, who was senior priest for Mugombwa Parish; and Father Eros, the youngest, who was always cracking jokes with everybody. Later during the 1994 Tutsi genocide, he had become the leader of their community in Nyanza. The Nyanza branch had been assisting orphans even before the genocide. While many other expatriates fled the country, Father Eros chose to stay with the children to protect them. At the end of the genocide, he was selected as someone who had saved many lives at his own risk. Presently, Father Eros is still helping orphans in the Nyanza community and remains a living model of boundless love.

To be admitted, I had to be very patient. The priests in this community proceeded to invite me to training sessions. They had to make sure that I was really able to live the life to which I was aspiring. After three years of training, those Italian priests invited me to sit for an exam for admission to Kabgayi Junior Seminary. Once at Kabgayi, I read Latin and other classes meant for junior seminary students, and I easily passed all the exams.

At Kabgayi Seminary, most of the trainees to priesthood belonged in the Kabgayi Diocese. I was one of the very few who wanted to be a priest in an international community. Father Giorgio Vito often visited me at the seminary, and he used to organize training for me and other young candidates during the holidays.

When I was getting ready to enter this community, Benjamin and Frodouard, who also aspired to this congregation and had meant to start religious life with me, changed their minds. We had started at Kabgayi Seminary at the same time and participated in the trainings together. During the period we spent together, they always assured me they had made up their minds for religious life, but they changed their minds in the last minute. Benjamin and Frodouard were from Gisenyi, President Habyarimana's prefecture, and they were always proud of their origin. They changed their minds about getting into the Rogationist community simply because the leaders were European, specifically Italian. They asked me, "How are you going to live with white people? You know, their culture is much different from ours." They tried to get me change my mind, and I really started to doubt myself. I decided to talk about it to my father during the holidays.

When I returned to my family, I was curious to know my father's position. One evening, I told him how my classmates had changed their minds, and that I would have to go alone. My father told me he found no problem there.

"I have been told that the white people's culture is very different from ours, you see. It is not easy to live with them," I answered.

"It is quite true; the white people's culture is very different from ours. Yet, theirs is not a hatred-based culture that would kill you or drive you out of your own country. Your classmates told you it was not easy to live with white men. Why should you seek an easy life?" my father retorted. Father's words and tone were hard and convincing.

I was happy with his advice and told him: "I agree with you, and I'll go alone. I am sure I'll find other people to make friends with." I started getting ready to leave my ordinary life and go far from my natural family for a religious life. Concerning my classmates, Benjamin got a job at a bank in his Ngororero while Frodouard went to the National University of Rwanda to further his studies. Neither of them had the interdictions which were mine, as Frodouard often told me: "You Tutsis have interdictions to further your studies or to access jobs." As for me, I got ready to enter a community where there were no prohibitions.

There was another group of young men from Mugombwa Parish studying at a school managed by the Salesians in Kimihurura, Kigali. They were, like me, aspiring to religious life with the Rogationists. Isidore and Alexandre were Tutsis; Charles, Jean, and Claver were Hutus. We trained together for religious life, but when they graduated from secondary school, only the Tutsis proceeded to religious life; the Hutus returned to normal life. Eventually, I found myself with the other Tutsis in the community: Alexandre, Isidore, and another young man called Damien. From the Hutu group, Charles went to a military school in Kigali; Jean taught at a secondary school in Mugombwa; and Claver attended the National University of Rwanda.

As seen at the beginning of this chapter, the motion from Rwandan Hutu students in Belgium concerning the socioeconomic issue then prevailing in Rwanda, wanted bishops of the local church to justify their position. Though I only talked of the situation in Mugombwa, the motion suggests that the imbalance was a fact all over Rwanda. In my opinion, it was easy to understand that situation, and those Hutu students in Belgium were perfectly aware of the fact, because many of them had gone to school in minor seminaries. Eventually, some of them had secured scholarships to the National University of Rwanda, and some others studied abroad. Their Tutsi classmates had no such opportunities. The only door left open to them was through the Church, meaning they agreed to be priests or members of religious communities.

With the system based on discrimination and injustice, which even interfered with the private decisions of the local church in my country, I was not proud to be a Rwandan. I wanted another identity, the identity of children from the Righteous Father, different from the "father of the nation." I needed a father of nations who bestowed his love on all of his children indiscriminately. To my knowledge, the Rogationist religious community was able to take me closer to this father, who would give me the identity I was looking for.

CHAPTER 6

RELIGIOUS LIFE
IN CYANGUGU

Choosing religious life was a way of seeking justice. My parents often told me that God was the only righteous who could defend us. Gradually, I have come to realize that they were right. The one thing remaining for me was to find ways to come closer to Him and enjoy the justice I was unable to get in the ordinary life of my country's political environment. I realized that religious life would help me get where I wanted to be. Indeed, all the religious people I knew lived in communities of different races and nationalities but were all united by faith in one God.

The Rogationist community was in Cyangugu, a town located in southwestern Rwanda, right at the border with the Democratic Republic of the Congo. Their house overlooked Lake Kivu, a very quiet place with a beautiful view of Bukavu City. This Cyangugu community was just a branch of the larger community in Rwanda and over the world. The congregation was founded by an Italian priest, Annibale Maria Di Francia from Messina City in Sicily. He was canonized and made a saint by Pope John Paul II in 2004.

In July 1989, I started training to be admitted to this international community. The training period was called a novitiate and lasted a whole year. After this year, I was to make one-year temporal vows, which were renewable until you took final vows. Ever since I started, I was always happy to lead a life that allowed me to live with people from different countries. Life in a religious community was very different from my previous life. I was to make a community life with people from other cultures. This was the kind of unity in diversity I was seeking.

Father Riccardo Pignatelli was the superior priest at the Cyangugu community. He was also master of the novices and superior-general of the Rwanda delegation. Father Arturo, another Italian, was the bursar. He was a good cook, and young people liked him for his meals. Whenever Father Arturo was preparing something in the kitchen, we all knew that the meal would be delicious. Besides excellent kitchen work, he was also good, sensitive, and very dynamic.

When I had spent a year with him in the community, he was appointed by his authorities in Rome to a community in Naples, and he left Rwanda for Italy. We were left with Father Riccardo, who became both superior priest and bursar. But from time to time, Father Eros, usually living in Mugombwa Parish, would come to help him whenever necessary.

Besides those Italian priests, there were Rwandan and Congolese young men in training. The first intake included Vénuste and Jean-Paul. But Jean-Paul later left to study in Rome, and Vénuste was left alone in his second year, which was devoted to the study of philosophy. There were four of us novices: François from the Democratic Republic of the Congo; and Patrice, Damien, and me, all from Rwanda. Another group of young men were awaiting admission to the novitiate. Some were Rwandan, and others were Congolese.

As we spoke different languages according to our origins, the regulation in the community was to speak only French. That was a good opportunity for me to improve my French. French was spoken by all, but we also had a class in Italian, taught by Father Riccardo. I liked this language so much that after his class, I always listened to conversations designed by specialists in the Italian language, using radio cassette players.

The core training was on spirituality, the life of our founding father, and the congregation regulations. Receiving explanations on the vows we were to take after completing the year was essential during that period. There were three vows: obedience, chastity, and poverty. Concerning the vow of obedience, Father Master explained how a good religious person was characterized by obedience in all humility to his superiors. Concerning the vow of chastity, not only friendly relationships conducive to sex were prohibited but thoughts opposed to this vow were also to be avoided. Concerning the vow of poverty, religious people were not allowed to have personal property like money or other goods without prior authorization from their superior. Prayer was an integral part of this training and was intensive.

In that life, I was disturbed by one thing: the schedule of the sacrament of reconciliation. Every fifteen days, I was to go to the confessional. It was a regulation, and a priest from the Barnabites regularly came to perform it. Before getting into religious life, I used to go to the confessional when I really needed it. With this new kind of life, I understood how difficult it was to find sins to be confessed within that time period. In reality, we were always together as novices in the community; our trips outside the convent were always organized. We traveled in groups to specific places. We had no visitors, besides our families who only came when it was really necessary.

Even if I was unable to find sins for confession every fifteen days, Father Master encouraged us not to miss confession. He told us we always made mistakes, and however small, they had to be forgiven.

He asserted that intentional sinning also needed regular confession. I often confessed intentional sins, because it was rare to find real sins. When I found nothing to tell the priest, I confessed kicking my colleagues during football matches. I also talked about the lack of order in my room, talking during practical work, and my lack of attention in the chapel during prayer.

I knew perfectly well that the year at the novitiate was a test, but it was impossible to compare it to the persecutions of ordinary life in Rwanda at that time. Within the community, ethnic-based discrimination and humiliation did not exist. I was sure that if I did well within a year, I would become a member of the international community, exactly like Western people. Then, I knew that ethnic quota was not a passport to access learning, and this was the one essential thing for me. Throughout that year at the novitiate, I had no particular problems, and eventually, I became a member of a religious order, taking renewable, one-year vows.

The vow-taking day at the end of the novitiate period was a great feast, and my father was invited for the ceremony. That very day, all of us new members of the congregation had new white frocks on, and the feast was well organized. When the superior admitted me as a community member, I was overjoyed. It meant that all such communities all over the world would be informed about it. I was aware that my new family was very large. The Rogationist congregation had branches in four continents: Europe, America, Asia, and Africa. I had won a big family that was more important to me than my nationality at that time.

My father could not go back home without showing his gratitude. During the feast, he made a good address of gratitude toward God and toward the Rogationist congregation. Some other parents to new members also made addresses, all thanking the congregation and its founder. The feast came to an end in a positive

49

atmosphere. It was especially positive for me, as I experienced my father's great happiness. At long last, he could contemplate his son in the community member's frock.

I finished the novitiate in July and had to start philosophy studies in September at the White Fathers' major seminary. The institute was across the lake in Bukavu, Democratic Republic of the Congo. It was a foreign country, but it only took me twenty minutes on foot to get there. Before beginning my studies, my superiors allowed me a two-week visit to my family. I particularly missed my mother, younger brothers, and sisters, as I had spent a whole year without seeing them.

I awaited the beginning of the philosophy program impatiently. In my community, Vénuste and Isidore had already started the program. Vénuste was to begin the third year, and Isidore was to begin the second year. To arrive at the major seminary, we first had to go through the customs on the Rwandan side; we crossed the Rusizi Bridge between Rwanda and the Democratic Republic of the Congo, four hundred meters from our destination. At the outset, we had no particular problem at the border. We were respected as religious trainees, and we went through without being checked.

I was pleased by my classes at the major seminary, especially by Introduction to Philosophy, Logics, and English courses. There were also classes in French and the Bible. Lecturers were mostly European: Belgian, French, Italian, and German. As philosophy students, we had a separate wing but took part in the morning, midday, and evening prayer, as well as shared meals with the other community members. To me, community life was ideal, and I was not sorry for choosing it.

The relationships between the government bodies and our superiors were excellent, and from time to time, we had visits from top authorities. One day, the then Minister of Youth, Colonel

BM Augustin Ndindiliyimana, came to our community to visit our superiors. Sometimes, the minister at the president's office, a native of Cyangugu Prefecture, also came for a visit. The prefect of Cyangugu and the Gendarmerie commander were our neighbors, and I often saw them in our house. Before those high authorities, I became a man of God rather than a Tutsi. I had started enjoying the advantages of my new identity and had no particular problems.

On October 1, 1990, the situation changed in the lives of Rwandans in general. In the evening, Father Riccardo called us and told us unusual news: "War has broken out in northern Rwanda. Tutsi refugees want to come back to their country. Don't be scared; we are far away from the battlefield." After his address, I panicked but did my best to hide my concern. I proceeded with my activities, my heart absent and elsewhere. Before going to bed, we went to the chapel for the evening prayer as usual, and we added special prayers related to this war. In silence, I supplicated God: "God our Father, protect us from this war, protect Rwandan people, the innocent Tutsis more particularly, likely to endure reprisals."

The following days, we went to the major seminary as usual until October 4. On October 5, a curfew was proclaimed all over Rwanda. We stayed in the community, and all businesses, schools, and public administration offices were closed ... everybody had to stay at home. Tutsis were arrested all over Rwanda and accused of complicity with the assailants. In Kigali more particularly, the Tutsis were massively arrested and gathered at the Nyamirambo Regional Stadium. They spent days and nights without food or water, and some had started eating grass to fight starvation.

In Cyangugu, the authorities started arresting Tutsis who were falsely accused of complicity with the RPF. It is this way that Marie-Paule, Jean-Paul, and their younger brother were arrested. The young people were ordinary citizens, fatherless and motherless. They were also devoted Christians, and when the administration started arresting the Tutsis, they fled to the Jesuit community. Many Tutsis were arrested, and the Cyangugu prison was full.

Concerning my family, I learned that my big brother Alexis had been arrested, beaten, and jailed in Butare. Many other Tutsis had been arrested there. They included Paul Gakuba, chairman of Mukura's football team, his brother Laurent Gatera, and his son Innocent Kayitare. My good acquaintance the rector of the minor seminary, Father Modeste, was arrested and jailed with the other Tutsi teachers at his school. All over Butare, the Tutsis were arrested, including teachers, tradesmen, and civil servants. My father was not arrested but told me he was permanently scared. Six months later and after negotiations, those Tutsis were released, but some of them had already died in prison: Paul Gakuba, Kamugunga, and others.

The RPF (Rwandan Patriotic Front) that had attacked northern Rwanda was composed of exiled Tutsis. But there were some Hutus like Alexis Kanyarengwe, a former influential collaborator of President Juvénal Habyarimana, Pasteur Bizimungu, and others. However, the Hutu extremists did not know about that Hutu presence within the RPF and said that the attack had been committed by Tutsis against Hutus. As a result, the Tutsis in general were considered to be in league with the RPF and were therefore considered enemies of the country.

The RPF attack was an occasion for the extremists to get rid of some undesired Tutsis. In Kibirira, the Tutsis were massively killed and 1,400 Tutsi civilians were reported killed at the beginning of the war. In the Mutara region, the Bahima, a clan of Tutsi pastoralists, were massacred, supposedly to avenge Hutu soldiers who had died at the front. In Murambi District, Byumba Prefecture, the Tutsis were massacred by Hutu extremists on the orders of the district burgomaster, Jean-Baptiste Gatete.

In our community, the situation was quiet. We were not subjected to searches, and nobody was arrested. To go to the major seminary, we had to cross the border and needed a document with the Cyangugu prefect's signature. In reality, this paper was easy to get for seminary students and religious people, because our Superior Father Riccardo was a respected man, and well acquainted with the prefect, who often visited our community. We went for the papers at the prefecture office, and they were delivered to each of us without delay.

The remaining problem was the military checkpoint and the screening of papers at the border. One day, I was going to the major seminary with Isidore and Venuste. We got to a military checkpoint that verified identity cards. They did not bother to ask me for my identity card. A soldier just abused me outright saying: "Go ahead, cockroach, I can see who you are; you're going to be in trouble with us soon." With my height and my general appearance, the soldiers could easily see I was a Tutsi.

Papers were asked from my colleagues, starting with Vénuste, who had no problem, as he was a Hutu. Isidore was more difficult to physically identify. From his physical features, the military had imagined he was a Hutu. Looking at his identity card, they found out he was a Tutsi. The soldiers were very angry: "Look at this one, also a Tutsi!" He was abused and verbally humiliated, but they let us go. Humiliated, we went our own way.

When we got to the border customs on the Rwandan side, harassment and abuse were waiting for me. On the Congolese side, one customs agent used to tell me whenever he saw me: "You, RPF fighter, we too are going to give you a lesson one day. If you do not stop coming this way, you are heading for trouble. You Tutsi are nasty. You'll see. We're going to drive you out of our land; we don't want you here!" I wondered why this Congolese guy was always so vicious with me!

Actually, President Mobutu of the DRC was a friend of President Habyarimana of Rwanda and had sent soldiers to help government soldiers fight the RPF. To be sure, the Congolese guy harassing me felt allied to the Habyarimana government. But to me, this was not a good enough reason to humiliate me daily. At that time, I could not lodge a complaint and had to endure in silence, and the daily humiliations were growing unbearable. I always thought this situation would pass and tried to find a way out, but I could not. Eventually, I realized that the only solution left was to entirely entrust myself unto God in my daily prayer.

My friend Jean-Pierre, a building site foreman in Cyangugu, used to tell me: "How come you cross the border every day, as tall as you are, and then return to Rwanda? Why don't you flee this country that persecutes the Tutsi?" I was skinny and tall, 1.87 meters, and this was enough to be considered in complicity with the RPF. Nearly every day, the soldiers humiliated me, and the border customs agents told me: "You cockroach, you're going to be in trouble one day on this border post." Harassed, humiliated, and abused, I could not see how I was going to go through my studies with those problems. And I had no alternative. I could not seek asylum in the DRC, as it would make no difference. Going back home to my village was worse. I had to stay in the community.

With the RPF attack, there was some positive changes politically, though persecutions against the Tutsis increased. In 1991, the Habyarimana government agreed to a multiparty system, and opposition parties were born. Most Rwandans were fed up with his self-interest seeking government. Every citizen did his or her best to find the means to live in dignity in the unfair country. On my side, I went on praying and was convinced that I was considerably contributing to the positive change in my country. In the community, I had enough time for prayer, and I entirely entrusted myself unto God, as I knew he was my only protector.

After a year of philosophy, I had learned important things that instilled more confidence and optimism. Professor Renis had convincingly taught me that absolute evil did not exist but that absolute good, God, existed. He taught me that worldly people are more attracted to particular goods, such as money, power, prestige, etc., disregarding or forgetting the absolute good. According to his explanation, evil is only a failure of the good; it can only exist in so far as it is related to the good. The one convincing example he used to give us was disease. Disease does not in itself exist; only sick people exist. We do not see tuberculosis but a person suffering from tuberculosis.

I had no difficulty understanding the prevalence of the absolute good over particular goods. Building on traditional belief in my country, I could easily identify names or proverbs that confirmed my professor's assertions. Some Rwandans are given such names as *Ntakirutimana,* or "there is nothing greater than God;" *Hakizimana,* or "only God saves;" *Bizimana,* or "only God knows;" and *Nahimana,* or "God is the last resort." Some of the proverbs include: *umwanzi agucira akobo Imana igucira akanzu,* or "While your enemy is digging a pit, God is opening up an exit door;" *Agati gateretswe n'Imana ntigahungabanywa n'umuyaga,* or "a tree planted by God laughs at the wind;" and *Iyo abanzi babaye benshi Imana iba mwene nyoko,* or "when there are too many enemies, God becomes your brother/sister."

Each time a Rwandan felt his or her end near, they would always call to God for help. This was also true for people who had never respected the absolute good: *Ntabara mana yanjye,* or "Oh my God, save me!" I never heard of anybody saying, "Money of mine, save me; ethnic group of mine or power of mine, protect me!"

The other lesson from my professor that helped me to better understand certain things related to the concepts of essence and accident in philosophy. He told us that being black, white, tall or short was an accident. These accidents do not exist in themselves but are always linked to essence, man. Though we belong to different tribes, ethnic groups, or races, we are all humans. Being human is more important than the particulars above, accidents that may be seen because humans exist. As the tendency of people is often to seek particular goods at the expense of the absolute good, they give more importance to accidents rather than to essence.

In the Rwandan situation at that time, to keep hold on their power and related interests, the Habyarimana government ordered the killing of innocent people, supposedly because they were of the same ethnic group as the RPF. Quite often, they just looked at a person's physical features, like height, and eliminated that person. My friend Jacques was a Hutu with the right identity card, but he was tall, and they killed him before verifying his identity. Though I lived as a member of a religious community, supposedly neutral, I was harassed, humiliated, and the military told me: "One day, we're going to make your long legs shorter."

Faced with these persecutions, I put my entire faith in God, whom I believed to be my absolute good. Besides daily prayer with the whole community, I used to pray by myself in silence on the road to and from the major seminary, especially because it was on this road that I met with the most difficulties. With these problems, I had started getting thinner, and I was permanently suffering from my belly. I often went to the hospital for treatment, but my health problems were endless. I lost weight on a daily basis.

A few months later, Father Arturo returned to Rwanda from Italy. When he saw me, he was surprised: "What happened to you, my son? You are so skinny …" He had known me before I joined the Cyangugu community, and he was worried about my health. He was aware that I was often going to the hospital but also realized I was making no improvement. One time, he called me and asked me a lot of questions about my health. He wanted to help me go to Italy for health care. I could see his compassion while I was answering his questions. He told me nothing, but I saw he was very thoughtful. After his stay in Cyangugu, he went back to Italy and started talking to his superiors in Rome about my case.

Cyangugu, on the day I took my first religious vows. From right to left: me, Father, and an uncle to one of my fellow friars.

CHAPTER 7

LEAVING FOR ITALY

One day, Father Riccardo abruptly told me that I was to fetch papers for a potential trip to Italy. Leaving Rwanda for Europe during those hard times was such a valuable gift. I had asked for God's help but had never contemplated such a solution. Superiors in Rome decided to send me to Italy for health care based on the information provided by Father Arturo. Father Riccardo, our superior at our Cyangugu community, did not understand why it was so necessary for me to go there for this purpose. I understood his hesitation perfectly well. As a superior, his duty was to avoid giving privileges to any of his friars.

"Everybody is asking me why you have to go to Italy for health care when you can get treatment in Rwandan hospitals," he told me. But the decision had been made at a higher level in Rome, and Father Riccardo had to obey.

"Go to the major seminary and ask the rector for transcripts. You may be able to continue studying in Rome," he told me. A few days later, he changed his mind.

"It is not necessary to ask for transcripts from the rector. I was told by Rome that your treatment may take only a fortnight. You will be coming back soon to Rwanda," he said.

"I already secured the transcripts; I fetched them as you had told me," I answered. I noticed that my superior was angry all of a sudden.

"You know, today another person asked me why you had to go to Italy when local hospitals can treat your disease," he retorted.

"Father, you know perfectly well that I went to more than two hospitals with no improvement. Taking this opportunity for health care in Italy away from me is going against the will of Providence," I said.

"I am not saying that you will not be going. You will certainly be leaving soon, but a few people keep asking a lot of questions concerning your case," he said. I noted that my superior was a bit confused on the subject of my departure.

Fortunately, one evening after the meal he told me: "Go to the district where you come from and fetch papers that will allow you to have a passport from the Ministry of Home Affairs in Kigali. You must go to Rome." I went together with Alexandre, a new religious recruit from my district. He had no passport either. Once at our district office, the secretary asked why we wanted the papers, and we answered that they were necessary for us to secure passports from the ministry. "You are lucky, as you are friars. Otherwise, it is not easy to get a passport if you are a Tutsi," he told me. I knew it well, but I also knew that there were a few exceptions to every rule.

Our superior was also informed of the difficulty of securing papers for Tutsis. So Father Riccardo, in his capacity as head of the Rogationist delegation in Rwanda, had prepared a letter of recommendation. The Cyangugu prefect, a man who enjoyed respect within MRND, the ruling party, gave us papers that accompanied and supported Father Riccardo's letter and the attestations we had secured from our district burgomaster. Actually, we had everything we needed to get a passport, unless bad luck prevailed.

In Kigali, the secretary general in the Ministry of Home Affairs, Callixte Kalimanzira, came from my parish and was a friend of my family. Before taking my papers to the ministry, I went to his place for advice, and he told me: "Take the papers to the Ministry, but

I am not sure you'll get a passport in these hard times." I was not discouraged by his words, and Alexandre and I took the documents to the ministry. When it was time to go and collect my passport, I was with Alexandre once again. With God's help, we found our passports ready. When I emerged from the office with my passport, a man I did not know came close to me.

"Tell me, how did you manage to get a passport?" he asked.

"I had nothing special to do; I just left the required papers …" I answered.

While I was explaining, he noted that I had a cross on my shirt and became quieter. Later he told me: "I see the reason why you had your passport without any problem, you are a man of God or a religious person! Because I am a Tutsi, I have spent several months after my passport, but they would not deliver it." He left, tears in his eyes, and I immediately realized how privileged I was. With my passport in my pocket, I had all the papers required for a flight to Italy. My superiors had now only to decide when I would leave. Meanwhile, Father Riccardo suggested just a short stay in Italy.

"You must go, but consider one thing: my fellow priests in Italy have assured me that your appointment had been taken at the hospital. I am sure you will be through in a fortnight, and you'll have to return soon for your studies with your colleagues."

"I agree with you. The one essential thing for me is to get treatment and recover my good health," I told him.

Before leaving for Italy, my superior allowed me to go to my family to say good-bye. Once in my village, I was amazed by the prevailing atmosphere at home and in the neighborhood. I went to visit my childhood friends, but I noted a change. At the school center where my father worked, all teachers knew me, and I considered some to be real friends. While I was trying to greet them warmly, I noted they were cold and responded as if I were a stranger to them.

When I spoke to them, they pretended not to hear. Faced with this mistrust and indifference from people I used to consider my friends, I was overwhelmed with frustration. I realized how hatred had overrun a major part of Rwanda.

I was disappointed and went to see my father to tell what I had just experienced. He was not surprised and said he was used to such attitudes. "Ever since the RPF attack in 1990, we Tutsis in this center have been marginalized. Only God protects us," Father declared. When I got home, my mother and sister confirmed the prevailing mistrust of our Hutu neighbors. I spent the night with my family but had no idea that it would be my last meal with my parents, my sister Marthe, and some of my brothers. Before going to bed, we prayed together, especially for the situation in our country. The following day, I hugged each good-bye, unaware that it was the last time I would ever see them.

I went back to my Cyangugu community to get ready to leave Rwanda. At long last, it was departure day. I had to be at Kamembe airfield not later than 2:00 p.m. The flight for Rome was very early the following morning, and the best alternative was to sleep in Kigali. I was going to board a small plane from Kamembe to Kigali and spend a night at the Hotel des Mille Collines. Fortunately, the cost of the hotel was included in my ticket. It was my first time spending the night in a hotel.

In the afternoon, Father Riccardo saw me to the Kamembe airfield. I was curious about the small fifteen-passenger plane. It was my first time travelling on an airplane. When I boarded the small thing, my expectations were for comfort and quiet during the trip. But at takeoff, I was scared. The mountain ranges in Cyangugu were dancing, and even Lake Kivu was restless. The higher the aircraft went, the more scared I became. Rather than enjoying the beautiful panoramic view of Bukavu City and Lake Kivu, I closed my eyes and started praying, expecting the plane to fall into the lake any moment.

Before going to Kigali, the plane was to stop in Gisenyi to take other passengers. While the plane was landing in Gisenyi, I tried to open my eyes but closed them immediately because houses and trees were moving up uncontrollably. Fortunately, the plane met no problems and remained on the tarmac, waiting for the passengers to board. I looked at the other passengers and noted how quiet they were, some even reading their newspapers, without a care. I was relieved and remembered that I had the same problems when I travelled in a car for the first time. Eventually, I came to the conclusion that there was no danger and that I simply had to get used to it.

From Gisenyi to Kigali, the weather was not good. It was very cloudy, and I felt the plane was in a mad dance due to frequent air pockets. I was even more scared, and my worries were even more acute than on the Kamembe-Gisenyi trip. I was only relieved by the other passengers' attitude. They were all quiet; they apparently had not experienced the same anxiety I had. Still, I was not entirely at peace.

Thank God! The plane safely landed in Kigali a few minutes later. Another difficult moment was the screening of passengers at Kigali Airport. I did not understand why the controlling agents kept me waiting, asking many questions while all the other passengers had already left. I noted the same scornful attitude that I had just left a few hours ago at the Rusizi border post between Rwanda and the Democratic Republic of the Congo. I thought they might arrest me and prevent me from going to Italy. Fortunately, my travelling documents were all right. At that time, to leave one prefecture for another, each Rwandan citizen had to have a traveling permit from his or her prefect. I had my permit, delivered and signed by the Cyangugu prefect, André Kagimbangabo. Better still, I had a cross on my jacket, a visible sign that I was a man of God. At that time, a man of God was more respected than other people.

The driver from the Hotel des Milles Collines was already waiting at the airport with a notice of his hotel. I got into his minibus, and we left for downtown Kigali. Once at the hotel, I had to take the elevator to get to my room. It was also my first time on an elevator. Fortunately, there were other people; otherwise, I would have been too scared. Once on the fourth floor, I left my luggage in my room and headed for the restaurant. I was warmly welcomed and given a good meal with nice, sweet music that helped me enjoy it. Eventually, I found the service very good, and I was at a loss for how to thank the God for that privilege.

Very early in the morning, the minibus was ready for the Kanombe airport. The plane took off about seven in the morning, and I traveled all day, praying for almost the whole trip. Indeed, on this Kigali-Brussels trip, and later on the Brussels-Rome trip, I was busy with one thing: my wish not to return to Rwanda. I asked God to give me words that would convince my superiors in Rome to let me stay in Italy. I did not want to go back so soon to my country's humiliation and frustration.

Once in Italy, I had a warm welcome from the community. Jean-Paul, a Rwandan citizen already living in the community, warned me that very early in the morning, we would go to the hospital to meet the doctor. The community had selected Francesco Bruno, a young Italian who was studying philosophy at the University of Lateran, to see me to Umberto I Hospital. Francesco had a sister working at the hospital. Her name was Rosaria, a nun and a doctor. Francesco and his sister did everything to make the experience perfect. Both were good to me, and I was very much relieved.

When the doctor saw me, his first comment was that I was suffering from a serious disease, as I was very skinny. He asked me to give all the required test samples for analysis. After a complete analysis, the doctor told me that all the test results were negative.

My major problem had been an aching belly and poor digestion. The doctor told me there was no indication of disease and that my problem might be psychological, but he had forgotten endoscopy in his analysis. Later, when I was no longer with the community, my doctor found out that I had been suffering from acidic reflux for years. This created digestion disorders that became worse in periods when I was under stress.

The doctor at Umberto I Hospital concluded that I had no problem. On the one hand, I was relieved not to be suffering from a serious disease. But on the other hand, I was worried because I had to go back to Rwanda, since there was no other reason to stay in Italy. One day, I talked to a priest and told him all about the difficulties I had in Rwanda. Sympathizing, he advised me to go and see the superior-general and explain my concern about returning to Rwanda.

With his advice, I asked for an appointment with Father Pietro Cifuni, superior-general of the worldwide Rogationist community. He granted me an appointment, and when I met with him, he welcomed me. I explained my concern about returning to Rwanda. After my explanations, the superior-general assured me I would not go back and that I would resume my studies in Italy. I was overjoyed and convinced that my prayers had been rewarded.

In the community, I started to learn Italian with the other young expatriates who aspired to religious life. Those young people came from different European countries. I had a great friend from Hungary called Stefano. His father was a farmer, and Stefano knew how to use a tractor to prepare the farm plots before planting crops. After Italian class, I would go with him to the plots to grow potatoes and vegetables. This hobby fetched admiration from the whole community and increased my chances to live with dignity in Italy.

I had some other friends: François from Mauritius, whose family lived in England; Vladimir from Poland; and David from the United

Kingdom. All those young people had been there before me and spoke a little Italian. In the community, there were other young people who were already going to the university but were with us in the evenings for prayers and the meal. They included one team from the Philippines, another team from Nigeria, two people from Zaire, three from Rwanda, two from South Korea, two from the Czech Republic, and one from Poland. There was also a large group of Italians that outnumbered the rest of us. I pushed hard to learn Italian in order to communicate with those young people who were always good with me. Thanks be to God! My Italian teacher congratulated me for learning very fast, and his words were very comforting to me.

Before going to Italy, my brother Alexandre had told me that religious people like people who take initiatives. Following his advice, I always sought something to do to actively participate in community life. As I had already started helping on the farm plots, I proceeded with this activity. The community had vegetable and fruit plots that were not properly taken care of. I decided to take care of them as much as I could. I collaborated with my colleagues at the community, but I was the only one to go to the farm plots, because the rest spent most of their time at the university. I had a lot of time and used it to make a strong contribution with my work. While the other friars were at the university, I went to the farm either for weeding, watering, or harvesting vegetables and fruit. In the community, there was an old priest who liked coming to the farm to see what I was doing and to provide advice. Thanks to my initiative, he had become a friend. When I had no Italian class, I would start my work at eight in the morning and finish about noon, when the other colleagues returned. I had a bath and ate lunch with the whole community.

Thanks to this work, I felt I was useful, and I ate my meals with a feeling of worth. Better still, my initiative won me respect from the entire community. When my colleagues found most of the farm plots taken care of and that vegetable production had increased, they congratulated me. My chances to have my visa extended also increased. Even if the superior-general had agreed to my stay in Italy, support from the Rome community was essential if I wanted to continue my religious life there.

From time to time, friars would take me to visit specific tourist sites in Rome. For a start, Jean-Paul, Damien, Louis, and Eloi took me to Saint Peter's Basilica. I was amazed by the number of tourists from all over the world who had converged on Saint Peter's place. The architecture of the whole basilica was very impressive and the interior wonderful. I had a feeling that the basilica was a creation of God rather than a building by human hands. That day, we also visited the Sistine Chapel, the Coliseum, and Saint John's Basilica in Lateran. All those places were fascinating and left a very strong impression on me.

More than anything else, I remember the interview with Pope John Paul II. While the bishops of Rwanda were in Rome, our superiors were informed and requested an authorization for us Rwandans to meet the pope. One day, one of our superiors informed us and advised to take the opportunity of the bishops' presence to see the pope and have photos with him. On that day, we went to the Vatican and first met the bishops from Rwanda. Then, we joined the room to wait for the Pope. When he arrived, he shook hands with every one of us while the photographer was taking photos. To this day, I keep this photo with Pope John Paul II jealously, and anyone who goes through my photo album asks how I had managed to have a photo with him.

I felt integrated into the international community in Rome. When I told my superiors that my visa was about to expire, there was no problem. I was immediately driven to a place that could extend it. God was still rewarding my prayers, and I was due to resume study in philosophy with my fellows at the University of Lateran.

At St. Peter's Square, Italy. From left to right:
me and my elder brother Alexandre.

CHAPTER 8

AT THE UNIVERSITY OF LATERAN

Eight months later in Rome, I was admitted to the second year of philosophy studies at the University of Lateran. Actually, as I had completed a year and a semester at the White Fathers Major Seminary in Bukavu, DRC. The University of Lateran validated the philosophy exams that I had passed there. I was registered at a great university, at long last! It had large and impressive buildings.

All continents were represented at the university, and I was impressed by the students who came from all over the world. There were people of all colors and types, and during the break, I loved contemplating that mosaic of people. The one thing that surprised me most was that you could not find any separatist, ethnic, or race-based problem. Far from the experience of ethnic-based discrimination in Rwanda, my only concern at the University of Lateran was to learn Italian well and to successfully complete my studies. Classes were taught in Italian, but for a better understanding, I also read books in French. Anyway, I was very motivated and morally strong.

Daily attendance was compulsory at the University of Lateran. From Monday to Friday, I got up very early in the morning, took part in the community prayer, and left for the University after breakfast. While the screening of papers was a daily routine when I was going to the major seminary in DRC, nobody in Italy ever asked for my identity card or any other document on the road or subway. I always met the police, but they were always polite and respectful in contrast to the soldiers I had left in Rwanda, at the hands of whom I had experienced a lot of verbal humiliation and abuse. This environment of respect was essential for my commitments. On the whole, this kind of atmosphere encouraged me and helped forget the humiliations I used to undergo in my own country before coming to Italy.

I had a small language problem but also the necessary force and determination for success. I worked hard every day and avoided any reason likely to send me back to Rwanda. I was curious to see how I was going to perform during the first sitting of exams. At the University of Lateran, most exams were oral. I had to be prepared to answer all the questions professors would ask me outright and face-to-face. I was used to written exams in Rwanda and the DRC and had to adjust to the new system.

Of all the professors in the Faculty of Philosophy, Professor Gian Franco Basti was the one we feared most—not because he was nasty but because he was very competent and demanding. He taught Philosophy of Anthropology, a course I found very interesting. His lecture notes included mathematical issues, which handicapped my understanding of the course. To avoid cutting a sorry figure, I did my best to get ready for the exam. I studied for Professor Basti's course every day.

When it was time for the first sitting of exams, my first scheduled exam happened to be Philosophy of Anthropology. I was confident and hopeful for a successful exam, as I had prepared, but I doubted my pronunciation of Italian. I was third on the list in that exam. When it was my turn, I came before my professor with a composed, confident attitude. He told me I could choose my language for the exam: Italian, French, or English, all of which he spoke perfectly. I gladly told him that I was going to answer in French.

For a start, I was to draw a question from the face-down pieces of paper on the table. Afterward, he asked me to read the question. Fortunately, I began well and convincingly. He asked more and more questions, and I answered with ease, and he probably realized that I had properly read his course. Eventually, he told me: "I can see that you have had a good preparation. I am going to ask you one last question, and if you answer very well, you will have all your marks." He asked the last question, which I answered faultlessly. As promised, he gave me *30/30 Lode*, that is, the maximum grade in the Italian system. He wrote it in my report book, and signed it.

Before I left, Professor Basti congratulated me and invited me to study philosophy up to specialization. I had never been so happy in my life. When I got out of the university heading for the subway, I was ecstatic, like a bird soaring. I could not understand how I had passed the exam with a maximum grade.

Once in the community, the other students were curious to know how I had performed. The first to see my report book was amazed and left immediately to show to everybody. None could understand what had happened, particularly because I did not speak Italian well. They did not know that I had answered in French. On my side, I was aware that I had done my utmost in preparing for that exam, but this did not prevent me from acknowledging God's continuous surprises to me. I left my bag and went to the chapel to show my gratitude to my creator.

Besides this exam, I had also passed all the rest with distinction and then felt that my situation in Italy was more secure. Furthermore, outside the university and the community, Italian people were very friendly, and their compliments gave me a sense of dignity I had not had in Rwanda. From time to time, I heard beautiful words from some Italians: *Tu sei alto e bello,* or "You are tall and handsome;" *Tu sei simpatico,* or "You are sympathetic."

During the Christmas period, I, Alexandre, also a Rwandan and a fellow friar, and Louis from the DRC, went to Messina. We had been invited by a family to share their meal. Sicilian people were constantly saying that we were handsome and sympathetic. Remembering how I had been called a serpent, a cockroach, or a vermin in my own country, I understood that hatred could change the beautiful into the ugly, the good into the wicked.

The Rogationist congregation had branches all over Italy. It was for me an occasion to visit the different tourist places in that beautiful country. The congregation headquarters were in Messina, the city where the founder father had started the community life of this religious family. I went to visit that community, and it was also a good occasion to go to Taormina and to Jardini-Naxos, two beautiful tourist sites on the sea shore. From there, you can see Mount Etna, a volcano that is still active. At different times, I visited Naples and Pompeii, Assise, Padua, Venice, and Milan. The one city that left the most impression on me was Venice, built at sea. For transport, people use boats or gondolas, and the city is full of tourists. Religious life gave me a break and let me forget the persecutions in my own country.

While my case was smoothly making progress in Italy, the situation in Rwanda was worsening every day. I learned the sad news that the Tutsis of Bugesera had been massacred. In Italy, most news was about an Italian volunteer, Antonia Locatelli, who had worked in Bugesera and had been killed because she had dared to denounce those massacres. It was March, and according to our superiors' decision, I was to return to Rwanda after my exams in June for a compulsory internship.

Another negative effect on my community life was the case of a countryman who had just left the community while he was bound to go back to Rwanda. He was to go there for a year's internship, but he did not like it. He opted for continuing his studies in Italy on his own. His attitude had made our superiors angry. Some said that it was no longer necessary for us to continue studies in Italy, and that we should go back home and study there. According to my superiors' opinion, Italy tempted us from going back home after graduation.

On the one hand, I could understand our superiors. They had invested in our studies for us to become well trained priests in their congregation. On the other hand, I was afraid to return to Rwanda during that period, which was so dangerous for the Tutsis. Besides the tension that existed between the Rwandan government and the RPF, the Tutsis in general were scared and for a good reason. Since 1990, the Tutsis had been massacred massively, especially in Murambi, Byumba Prefecture, Kibirira, Bugesera, and Mutara. I was particularly scared of the impunity that prevailed after the massacres. Everybody knew who the perpetrators were. One of the most infamous was Jean-Baptiste Gatete, burgomaster of Murambi district. Rather than being prosecuted for his crimes, he was given a promotion. Only after the genocide was he sentenced by the International Criminal Tribunal for Rwanda in Arusha.

There were many signs at that time showing that the Tutsis were seriously threatened in Rwanda. I was informed that one extremist political party, the Coalition for the Defense of the Republic (CDR), had just been created. From time to time, members of this party would kill a few Tutsis in total impunity. Straton Byabagamba was a good example. He was a Catholic journalist who was killed in his home in Kigali. My big brother Alexis had nearly escaped death at Kirarambogo and had to spend the night in a papyrus forest to run away from members of CDR. Those extremists who were after his life feared nothing and were preparing other crimes. My cousin Augustin told me in his letter that the extremists openly boasted that they were just waiting for a signal to exterminate the Tutsis.

Concerning this situation in my country, there was a big misunderstanding between us Rwandans and our superiors. For the latter, refusing to go back to Rwanda was a kind of caprice caused by the attraction of the high standard of living we were offered in Italy. For me, staying in Italy was a matter of survival, and I was aware that I could not start a debate on this subject: "Do not let yourself be led astray by the good life in Italy," my spiritual father used to repeat to me. Worse, a countryman of mine had just left the community after he tried to negotiate with our superiors about making his religious life in Italy instead of returning to Rwanda. The answer had been negative.

Before definitively deciding whether I was to return home or not, I wrote a letter to my cousin living in Cyangugu to ask about the prevailing situation. He worked at the Cyangugu Tribunal, and I was sure he monitored the country politics on a daily basis. I informed him that I was about to return to Rwanda, and his letter was hard: "Dear cousin, the situation here is very dangerous. As you have been lucky enough to leave Rwanda and get into Europe, don't come back now, please. You may be the only one to survive. We are unsafe here. We do not even know whether we shall be living tomorrow. Take this opportunity offered by Providence and stay where you are." My cousin's words were so strong that my nights were visited by nightmares for a whole week.

After this letter, I started to seek a solution to the problem. As said above, I was unable to ask my superiors for authorization to stay in Italy. This alternative was to be excluded and I had to find a solution outside the community. Leaving the community was also very painful. Staying in Italy outside the community was not secure. Going elsewhere in Europe was very difficult. I had to find a solution quickly, but I knew one thing: I was not going back to Rwanda.

I was not the only one who did not want to go back. Another friar, Damien, was doing everything to stay in Italy. He was a dynamic type, and when he wanted something done, he would put all his energy into it and quickly found a solution. I often talked with him about the situation in our country, and we knew it was dangerous to return at that time. Each of us was trying to find a personal answer to this question.

One day, Damien came to see me and said, very happily: "I found a place to stay. I found a community that agreed to help me resume my studies in Italy. I am worried for you, but I hope God will also help you." He told me what he had done: he had talked to a professor of his. The latter had advised to simply inform his superiors. Damien left, assuring me he would pray for me.

Two days later, I went to see Damien in his room. It was about four in the afternoon. I knocked at his door, and there was no answer. I knocked again, and he did not respond, but I knew he was inside. I opened the door and found Damien stretched out on his bed, crying. I asked what had happened, and he did not answer. A few minutes later, he said: "I told my superior everything, and everything is a mess now. He is furious with my decision." I tried to ask what exactly the superior had told him, but Damien would not tell me. Eventually, he said: "It's all over now. I must return to Rwanda. There is no other solution."

Damien's case confirmed the impossibility of negotiating with my superiors to stay in Italy. They were furious with anyone who tried to stay. I really understood them, but I would not go back to Rwanda. I decided to manage my business secretly, in spite of a major problem: how to get out of the community without saying good-bye? I had to find an appropriate way to leave discreetly, without confrontation. But to close Damien's case, he had to return to Rwanda, and we learned later that he had been killed.

The acquaintances I could share my concern with included one Rwandan student in Switzerland. I wrote a letter to him explaining my worries about going back to Rwanda. He understood my problem and responded positively. He told me he was going to try to get a two-month sponsorship for a stay in Switzerland, waiting for a more sustainable solution to be found. When I read the letter, I was happy and imagined that I would find a solution within two months. He sent sponsorship papers to me, and I went to the Embassy of Switzerland. I was given a visa without problem.

While the other Africans were getting ready to go back home, I was getting ready to go to Switzerland. To get out of the community, I informed my superior that before going to Rwanda, I wanted a permission to honor an invitation from friends in Switzerland. He rejected my request outright and told me I had to go to Rwanda without trying to find a pretext. After this interview, I realized that the situation was complicated, and that I had to change my strategy. Before deciding how to leave the community, I devoted enough time to intensive prayer to ask for God's company in a new project.

A few days later, I had a good idea. I called Father Arturo, who was staying in Aquilla, and asked him to welcome me into his community, as I needed his advice on my current problems. Without hesitating, Father Arturo said he was waiting for me in his community. He had certainly talked to my Rome superiors, because I was allowed to go and see him at Aquilla before going back to Rwanda. I left the community, but instead of going to Father Arturo's community, I headed for Termini Station to take a train to Switzerland.

While waiting at the station, I was restless, my soul sad. I imagined that someone from the community would be there to prevent me from going. Worse, I felt guilty for leaving my community that way. I had time before departure, and I went to a church near the station. I got on my knees, and I entrusted my worries unto God. After this prayer, I felt relieved. I took my traveling bag and left for Switzerland.

CHAPTER 9

MY SHORT STAY IN SWITZERLAND AND A NIGHT IN PADUA

My friend lived in Fribourg City. When I got there, he welcomed me. Before doing anything else, I called Rome to inform them that I had left the community and that I was in Switzerland. The priest who answered my call was surprised to hear that. He told me that I had made a serious mistake and had to come back to Rome immediately, but I could not go back there. My religious life with the Rogationists was over. I politely answered that I had made up my mind about leaving the community once and for all to resume my ordinary life.

I regretted this way of leaving the community, especially lying to Father Arturo. Later, he was suspected by the Rome community for complicity in my action, but he absolutely knew nothing about it. Father Arturo was sad, and when I called him, he recognized me and said with anguish: "Father Arturo is not around," and I immediately understood that he did not want to talk to me. I was also sad but had no other way to leave the community, and I could not afford to tell the truth about my project!

I spent two days in Fribourg with my friend before going to Valais Canton, where I was to stay in a family. My friend had talked to a Rwandan family living there, and they had agreed to take me for two months. Their family consisted of a father, a mother, and a six-year-old child. The father was a medical doctor doing his specialization in Valais Canton, and his wife was a nurse studying in Geneva. She came home at weekends. From Monday to Friday, I was by myself at home doing household work. The child went to school while his father worked at a clinic.

I knew I had to be useful in order to avoid overburdening my hosts. In the morning, I arranged the house, sometimes did the washing and the ironing, saw the child to school and back home after school, and did the cooking. They were happy with my contribution to everyday work, and sometimes during the weekends, we would visit other members of the Rwandan community in Geneva. With the latter, there was only one subject of conversation: the issue of security in our country. Quite often, the Swiss Television showed pictures of the aftermath of the war between the RPF and the Rwandan government. At Nyacyonga, a few kilometers from Kigali City, there was a large camp for Rwandan refugees who had fled the war in northern Rwanda. Those refugees lived in miserable conditions and inspired anger and anguish to anyone who saw them. With the pictures, I realized that there was no peace in my country and did not regret not returning there.

From time to time, I called my friends in Italy to negotiate ways to resume study there. I had a doctor friend, a member of an association that worked in Rwanda. His name was Maurizio. I got acquainted with him for the first time when he was in Rwanda with his wife Sonia. They had come to my Mugombwa parish with a team from the association to visit their projects in the parish. As I lived in the Mugombwa community at that time, we shared our daily meals during their stay, and in the end, we became friends. We used to write to one another after their return to Italy. While I was in Rome, I visited the Padua community with the other Rwandan friars. During our stay there, Dr. Maurizio learned I was in Padua and invited me to his home for a meal.

From Switzerland, I called and informed him that I had left the Rogationist community and was seeking another way to resume my studies. He did not hesitate and said: "You may come to Padua and do your studies here. I must take my holiday and leave now, but we shall talk about it later …" After this exchange, I was sure to study in Padua. Besides Dr. Maurizio, I talked to my other acquaintances, and some of them let me know that studying in Italy was possible. After making the contacts, I stayed quiet, waiting for the end of the holiday in late August to return to Italy.

Meanwhile, an Italian family in Sicily I used to know invited me for a short period at Taormina. I had just spent a month in Switzerland, and I found it appropriate to accept their invitation. Before leaving Switzerland, I thanked my friend and the family that had welcomed me and left for Taormina. Once there, I received a warm welcome from the Nelso family, an old couple living alone. They were devout Catholics and went to church daily. Thanks to this family and other friends, I was acquainted with Father Filippo and Achille, who also bestowed their friendship on me. With all these acquaintances, my worries were over, and I was certain I would not go back to Rwanda without my consent.

Dr. Maurizio's holiday was over, and I was to go to Padua and talk to him about my studies. Actually, I preferred Padua City over Messina. I went there to hear what Dr. Maurizio had to say, but I had forgotten he was a friend and collaborator of the Rogationists, and that we had known each other thanks to them. He could not help me without asking my former superiors, and unfortunately, my unauthorized leave had aroused their anger. So, when I got in Padua, I noted that Dr. Maurizio had changed. He was with two men I had also met in Rwanda: Dr. Marco and another one whose name I could not remember. They were all members of the aforementioned association.

When I came closer to greet them, I had prepared to embrace them warmly as usual, but they hardly touched my hand. I immediately understood I was not welcome. They asked me to go with them to a restaurant and they ordered drinks and food. Dr. Maurizio was the first to ask me a question.

"Did you talk to your Rome superiors before coming here?"

"No, I did not, as I am not under their orders anymore. I have left the congregation once and for all," I answered.

"Why did you go without their authorization, then?" he asked again.

"Because they would not allow me to stay in Italy," I said. He went on asking me why I did not want to go back home. When I said it was because of security issues in my country, he said I was not right, because the parties in conflict had signed the Arusha Peace Accord.

After this exchange, I was unable to eat the pizza they had bought for me. They were all angry, and Dr. Maurizio tried to convince me that I had disobeyed. "You have disobeyed those who brought you to Italy, and we have no guarantee either that you are not going to disobey us." On the whole, I knew that Dr. Maurizio was right and that he had talked to my former superiors in Rome.

Before putting an end to our exchange, he asked me two questions.

"Don't you have any other possibility of staying in Italy?"

"No. I said good-bye to my friends in Taormina, and I have no other alternative," I said. He asked the last question.

"Why didn't you stay in Switzerland, then?"

"It is not at all easy to stay in Switzerland. I had a visa for only two months, but my stay in Italy is still valid …" I answered.

"Okay, we too are going to proceed like Switzerland and reduce the amount of time foreigners are permitted to stay. Now sir, we talked to your superiors in Rome, your ticket is ready. You're going to Rome tomorrow to get ready to go back home. The only thing we can do for you is call Father Tiziano to pick you up at Kigali Airport." I felt cheated after Dr. Maurizio's words, but after a minute's thought, I gathered myself.

"Doctor, when I came here, I hoped you were going to help me stay away from Rwanda. If you think there is no risk, I am ready to go home. I'll go to Rome tomorrow to collect my ticket and go back to Rwanda."

"Good. We are going to show you your room at the hotel, and we wish you a nice trip back home," he said. They saw me to the hotel and said good-bye.

I was sad but hoped my Italian friends in Messina were not going to let me down like those in Padua. Before going to bed, I called the Nelsos' home in Taormina to ask for Father Achille's telephone number. Mrs. Sebastiana answered and told me: "You have done well to call. Father Achille has been looking for you, and we did not know how to find you. Please come back quickly tomorrow and go talk to him." I was relieved and went to bed a confident man. It was in September, only seven months before the Tutsi genocide started in Rwanda.

When I got to Taormina the following day, they presented me with a letter of Father Achille's inviting me to a meeting with other young people who aspired to priesthood. During this meeting, I had an opportunity to talk to him. He encouraged me to proceed on the way to priesthood and assured me I would get there. Father Filippo, senior priest at the Graniti parish, was also there and had the same opinion as Father Achille. Both advised me to start theological studies to determine if I still really had a calling for priesthood. For me, the single most important thing was to stay away from Rwanda, and their proposition was not opposed to my purpose. Obviously, my answer was positive.

Father Achille was to introduce me to the archbishop of Messina before starting my theology studies. He asked for an appointment, which was granted. I traveled with both priests. Once there, the priests went first and talked to the archbishop in his office. When they finished, I went there, too. Actually, the archbishop did not ask me many questions. He simply showed he was happy to welcome me at Messina. With the interview, my nightmares were over, and I could stay in Sicily in peace.

For accommodation, Father Achille and Filippo sought a community, the Venturini Fathers. They lived in Barcellona Pozzo di Gotto, a few kilometers from Messina. The community included Superior Father Valentino; Father Angelo, and Father Roberto. Father Joseph from Cameroon was staying there as a student. He was about to graduate and return to Africa. The community often welcomed people for short prayer retreats. It was a quiet place, far away from the noise in the city. I was to stay there for a year of reflection as part of my calling to the priesthood while studying theology. But my active involvement in the religious life of the Venturini was a condition to go on living in their community.

There was another candidate to the priesthood with me. His name was Felipe, from Chile. He too was recommended by Father Achille. Discipline was a must in the community. We were to take part in prayer with the priests, prepare the hymns, and daily mass. Sometimes, I stayed at the reception area to welcome visitors and answer the telephone. The superior was to report to the archbishop on my behavior. He had the authority to give a go-ahead for my definitive admission to the Messina major seminary. But before this decision was made, I was studying my first year of theology at Saint Thomas Salesian Institute.

CHAPTER 10

HORROR OF THE GENOCIDE

On April 7, 1994, I left as usual for St. Thomas Institute in Messina, a branch of the Salesian University in Rome. I had started studying with the faculty of Theology in October 1993. Once there, a young man who was not in my class came running to me and said: "Do you know Hormisdas, the presidents of Rwanda and Burundi have just been killed. In Kigali, hunting down the Tutsis is the main event." A sudden shiver ran through my whole body. I realized that the awaited signal to exterminate the Tutsis was there. I entered the classroom but was unable to concentrate that day. I was thinking of my family but could not go out and make a call because my relatives lived in the village without a telephone. I was disturbed and at a loss.

When I came back to the community at two o'clock, I immediately headed for the television room. The headlines were about the killing frenzy that prevailed in Rwanda, hunting down the Tutsis, especially in Kigali City. According to the news bulletin, roadblocks were established all over Rwanda, and all the borders were closed to stop the enemy. I knew perfectly well that the so-called enemy referred to the Tutsis. Indeed, since the RPF attack in 1990, the Tutsis were considered enemies of the country.

President Juvénal Habyarimana, the "Father of the Nation," had just been killed. But he had also left a heritage of hatred that was beyond measure. In Rwanda, heirs would normally enjoy the heritage entirely following the death of their benefactors or parents. Before he was killed, President Habyarimana had long trained the *Interahamwe* militia, young Hutus from his MRND party. Those young people were well trained and equipped with weapons. Guns, grenades, and a lot of machetes had been distributed among the civilian population. Sources like Radio Télévision Libre des Mille Collines (RTLM) had already been propagating hatred against the Tutsis. The one thing remaining for the heirs was to implement what they had been learning for thirty years. As a reminder, killing a Tutsi had not been a crime since 1959. In April 1994, it was the final solution, first in Kigali. And a week later, the Tutsi were being killed all over Rwanda, regardless of age or sex.

In Butare Prefecture, southern Rwanda where my family lived, the extremists had not yet started killing, because the prefect was a Tutsi. On April 19, 1994, Théodore Sindikubwabo, interim president and native of Butare, traveled there to sensitize the killers. In his speech held at Butare Multivalent Hall, he said that people in that prefecture were behaving as if they were not concerned by the events then taking place all over the country. He called them *nyirantibindeba,* or "the indifferent ones." Afterward, the extremists in that place also started to "work" toward the extermination of the Tutsis. In Butare-Ville, their first victim was the prefect, Jean-Baptiste Habyarimana and his whole family. As a Tutsi, he had attempted resistance against the genocide. After his death, the killings were widespread throughout Butare Prefecture, to the remotest villages.

Besides the information from the television, I had no other means of knowing what was happening in my country. Fortunately, my brother Alexandre had been able to escape before the massacres and was in Bujumbura. Their superior had decided to flee with the whole community toward Burundi. They had also taken along my other brother Alexis and his son Ennode, who had been staying at Kabutare Hospital. Once in Bujumbura, my two brothers received the rare Tutsis who had been able to escape. My younger brother Godefroid was among them. He was the only member of my family in the village who had been able to escape, at night. He then hid in the papyrus marshland and crossed the Akanyaru River to Burundi.

One afternoon, as I was watching television, Father Valentino called me: "There is a call for you from Africa." I ran to the telephone booth. It was my brother Alexandre. And he told the bad news: "Our parents, four brothers, and two sisters were killed on April 22, 1994. Please be strong. The massacres did not only target our family. The Tutsis were being killed all over Rwanda …" I was unable to speak and remained quiet on the telephone. My brother guessed that I was unable to proceed with the conversation and eventually said: "Be strong and courageous. Good-bye." When he hung up, I was not strong enough to leave the telephone booth. I did not know what to do. I could not understand what had happened to my family. It was horrible. The apocalypse that had been announced by the extremists had begun.

There were twelve of us in our family: two parents and ten children. Thank God! Only four had survived: Alexis, Alexandre, Godefroid, and me. The following were killed:

My father, Siméon, sixty;

My mother, Odette, fifty-eight;

My eldest brother, Francois, forty; and his wife, Spéciose. They had four children: the oldest was fifteen, and the youngest was two. Miraculously Francine, who was seven at the time, was the only one to survive.

My sister Bernadette, thirty-six; her husband, François, and
their four children. No one survived.

Antoine, twenty-nine, and his wife, Cécile. She was four months
pregnant.

My younger sister Marthe, twenty-seven. According to multiple
sources, her death was atrocious. She was raped by several
militiamen before she was killed;

Emile, twenty-five; and Michel, sixteen.

For a long period, I was visited by my dear family's spirits.
In all places—the community, the streets, or the classroom, I
imagined scenes of their death, and the images would not let go.
On television, the news and the pictures from my country would
revive my pain. It was there: the genocide of the Tutsis was a fact,
and soon, the international media used this term. Men, women,
children, old people, the physically disabled, and the sick were all
killed. You just had to be called a Tutsi. The killers said they were
avenging their dead president, allegedly killed at the hands of the
RPF rebel army, most of whom were Tutsi. The genocide went
on. Hutus relentlessly hunted down the Tutsis hiding in the bush
or in marshlands. The RPF was fighting the government army in
a desperate attempt to save some hypothetical Tutsis who might
be still living.

The people who lived with me asked what was happening in
my country, but I was unable to explain in Italian. I needed to talk
about it in Kinyarwanda, my mother tongue. Unfortunately, no one
in my community or even in Messina could speak it. I was the only
Rwandan there, maybe in the whole of Sicily. I had never heard of
any Rwandan in the region. Rather than answer their questions,
I was confused and decided to leave them and stay alone. I went
upstairs to my room but could not stay there either.

I took a few minutes for reflection. I went down to the television room to get more from the daily news bulletin. The RPF was winning more ground, and many Hutus were already fleeing. There were pictures of many refugees in Zairean camps, and cholera had already claimed many victims. Nyiragongo Volcano was also in the news. It was known to be active, but this time, it was angry and ready to erupt. There were signs that lava would soon be projected onto the refugees. And journalists made comments that even nature did not accept those Rwandans.

Listening to the news and watching those pictures, my fellows in the community were affected and very compassionate toward the refugees. I had no pity. Rather, I was angry and bitter. A priest who was watching television told me: "How come these innocent people are suffering this much while the RPF are winning more ground?"

"Those refugees in front of you are not innocent; their hands are bloodstained. At least, they were able to flee while my relatives were hunted down like wild animals, tortured, and killed with no one coming to rescue them," I answered. After this answer, he calmed down.

"I understand your grief now, but do not forget that there are children and other people who did not take part in the genocide," he said. After this, I went out to the garden. I did not want to continue the discussion.

In the garden, the images of refugee camps kept coming to my mind as I walked. I contemplated the camps and the volcano nearby and talked to myself loudly: "Why doesn't it project its lava onto the camps for all to perish under fire?" Concerning cholera, I wished the assistance would take more time to arrive for the refugees to die massively. In my imagination, the war had broken out, and I was enacting it. I said, "Puff, puff," as if I were firing on people. In my burning mind, I wanted a machine gun to kill all the Hutus indiscriminately. Fortunately, someone was watching me from his room upstairs. He came down immediately to see me. Even before getting close he said: "My dear, you'll go mad." It was Father Domenico. He asked me to sit down on a bench in a corner to talk about it.

Father Domenico proceeded to teach me.

"My son, I know you lost almost all of your family. I know you are in a very tight situation, but if you do not take care, you shall go mad! Allow me to ask you one thing. How did you come here?"

I kept quiet and thought for a few minutes, and then, "Father, I came here fleeing the persecutions in my country, but I did not know they would grow into genocide," I answered.

"Thank you! You said it so well: you were running away, and you are now protected. I know you are not persecuted here. Please, think about your survival. Remember the hard times you went through before you came here. Do not forget all the kindness you received, and thank God because you are alive," Father Domenico said.

While he was speaking, Mr. Angelo, his wife, and their daughter Myriam arrived to greet us. They had overheard the subject of our conversation. The priest changed the subject: "Dear Hormisdas, with this genocide, the Rwandan people proved to us that they were still at least five hundred years behind where human progress is concerned." He went on to explain how genocide could not be accounted for, but I was not listening. The words he had said about thanking God for keeping me alive were still in my mind. They reminded me why my father had given me the name of Ndayishimiye and everything he used to tell me as linked with this name. Meanwhile, the Angelo family had left. A few days later, I met Myriam and her mom. They told me the conversation between me and Father Domenico was very interesting. Father Domenico, seeing I was lost in thought, also left. But before that, he asked me to continue thinking over what he had said.

I was left on my own in the garden, meditating on my parents' words to me when I was still with them. I was especially meditating on the persecutions of the Tutsis but also on the kindness I received during this period. In January, three months before my father was killed, he wrote me a very beautiful letter, as he had never written before. I was most affected by the words in his conclusion: "My son, you are not alone, we are always with you in our daily prayer ... I bless you and may God forward my benediction." With this reminder, I also remembered that my father used to warn me against hatred and to ask me to practice gratitude.

I was surprised that Father Domenico had just repeated the same recommendations as my father. A Rwandan saying teaches the following wisdom: *Ujye utinya icyo abagabo babiri bavuze,* or "Heed a word proffered by two wise men." My father's words on gratitude and warning against hatred had been repeated by Father Domenico. Thinking it over, I was convinced this was not only my father's heritage but also the highest command from God our Father. For me, gratitude if used to fight hatred was also a great sign of love.

After twenty minutes of meditation on all the kindness I had received so far, I found myself a privileged person rather than a wretched one. I found my survival to be a great gift. The extremists had killed most of my family and practically most of the Tutsis. As a true heir of my father's, I realized how big my responsibility was. My heart was suffused with the duty of gratitude, like my father's in his difficult moments. I then realized that bitterness, resentment, hatred, and vindication would not be important for me anymore. In future, I would be keeper of the values of gratitude and faith as taught by my father. I was convinced that he had received them from God our Father. I had no doubt about it; though I was aware of how difficult it was to implement them constantly during these times, it was yet critical.

Fortunately, I had enough force, based on my commitment, to jealously keep my communion with God. I was aware that God had helped and protected me so much against the Hutu extremists' frenzy. I knew the hatred that had already invaded me would deprive me of this communion, and I made up my mind to fight it with all my might. Thanks to Father Domenico's reminder, my bitterness subsided, and I continued to think positively about my future.

I left the garden relieved, but the scene of my relatives' atrocious deaths would not leave my mind. I knew those innocent people were wiser and better than I was. I went back to my room, and I still wondered what I had done to escape the horror and misery that had swept down onto my country. This gave me still more strength and courage to overcome my spiritual wretchedness and protect my mind's health. I had to fight bitterness constantly, because anger would regularly come back, and I would wish the killers evil. Anyway, I was not the same person as at the beginning of the genocide, and I knew daily struggle against hatred would continue. Though I was making progress concerning gratitude and the healing of my soul, provocations from the extremists were frequent. According to the information I could get, the Hutu extremists were trying to justify their wretched acts, alleging the genocide was the result of an angry population who had just lost their president. But I knew perfectly well: this genocide was the outcome of a culture of hatred toward the Tutsi that had begun thirty-five years earlier. Fortunately, rather than making me bitter, those allegations made my determination still stronger to avoid the hatred nurtured by those killers.

With this determination, I was strong enough to continue studying theology. Almost all of my classes came back over and over to God's love for us, especially through the sending of his only son, Jesus Christ. The kind of love suggested by Jesus (Matthew 5: 43–48) was very different from our selective love:

As the disciples had gathered around Jesus on the mountain, he said to them: "You have heard that it was said, 'You shall love your neighbor and hate your enemy.' But I say to you, Love your enemies and pray for those who persecute you, so that you may be sons of your Father who is in heaven. For he makes his sun to rise on the evil and on the good, and sends rain on the just and on the unjust. For if you love those who love you, what reward do you have? Do not even the tax collectors do the same? And if you greet only your brothers, what more are you doing than others? Do not even the gentiles do the same? You therefore must be perfect, as your heavenly Father is perfect."

I totally agreed with this passage and was not entitled to oppose God's word, my absolute good and provider of all blessings. I realized that my first duty as a Christian was unconditional love for others, including my relatives' killers. I realized the difficulty in my responsibility, but I knew God was going to help me. I was sure he had made me leave Rwanda before the genocide and that he would give me strength enough to completely overpower the temptations of resentment and revenge. Treating my relatives' killers as my brothers in Christ was part of my duty. And my contribution to their conversion was necessary.

CHAPTER 11

LOVE AND COMPASSION IN SICILY

While I was growing self-reliant, I also felt that God was with me through the Italians of Messina. Gradually, I started experiencing unconditional love and boundless compassion from those people. Messina is in Sicily, a region which used to frighten me, because I had been told it was a mafia stronghold. But it became for me a place of consolation in that very difficult period. Every acquaintance of mine asked what he or she could do for me. I did not have any answer and kept silent. I was not yet able to take initiatives. Seeing that I was unable to respond to the generosity of Sicilians, Christian people who used to come frequently to the community organized something. They had plenty of ideas. One day, Father Valentino called me to say that some Christians had proposed to help me go and meet my surviving brothers who were then in Bangui, in the Central African Republic.

What a wonderful idea! With the proposition, I felt more relieved and accepted that divine intervention. Besides my Christian acquaintances, students at Saint Thomas mobilized themselves to collect money for my trip. Father Tindaro, senior priest at St. John the Baptist parish called me to say that the members of his parish had something for me. Di Pietro's family used to invite me quite often to spend some time with them. They wrote me a beautiful letter in which Di Pietro's wife told me their house was my house, and they would be very happy to have me any time I wanted to be there. She also said she and her husband were my parents and their children, Laura and Carlo, were like my sister and brother. This letter went straight to my heart. It gave me the one thing I needed most: a family.

Everything necessary for the trip was ready soon. A few days later, I boarded the plane for the Central African Republic through Paris and a stop in Douala, Cameroon. Once in Bangui, my brother Alexandre was at the airport to meet me. Once I got to the refugees, I was curious to know how my sister-in-law Agnès, my big brother's wife, had survived. I also wanted to know what had happened to the other members of my family. Actually, Agnès had been miraculously saved. Here is a summary of her testimony in the next three paragraphs.

With her baby strapped on her back and my sister Marthe, they ran to hide in Kirarambogo Health Center when the killings started. They spent a night there, and during that night some Hutu extremists informed them they had just killed my parents, who had refused to leave their home. The following day, Marthe decided to go and hide with a family friend, Gérard's. Gérard is the same very man who had saved my father in 1959. Unfortunately, the extremists were informed, and the militia leader himself went to fetch and bring her to the health center. When Agnès saw her for the last time, she was supplicating that leader to kill her without torture. The killer immediately led my sister to an unknown place, and Agnès did not know what followed.

After my sister's deportation to an unknown place, the killers gathered all the terrorized Tutsis, women and children who had found refuge in the center, and took them to Akanyaru River. Agnès was in that group meant to be thrown into the river. Before they were led to their execution place, the victims were first stripped of their clothes, and their hands were bound. They were beaten up all the way to Akanyaru. They came close to a water point where people were drawing water. Agnès was very thirsty and asked one of the people she knew for some water. Rather than giving the water, she teased her, saying she would be having all the water she wanted in a few minutes, it being plenty in Akanyaru River.

Agnès was carrying her little daughter strapped on her back when they got to the river. The executioners started killing their victims first before throwing them into the river. When her turn was close, she threw herself into the river, her baby still strapped on her back. She fell on her back but did not go deep into water. When they saw that she did not drown, one of the militiamen took a canoe oar and started hitting Agnès on her head. The only thing she remembered was that she passed out. She then came to find herself held by the grass. By miracle, she was at the opposite river bank, on the Burundian side, but her baby had been carried away by the river. She was not strong enough to leave the place, and she stayed there. Good Burundi Samaritans found and took her to the nearest health center. Agnès was taken care of, and later, my brother Alexandre, who had learned the good news, fetched her to Bujumbura to join her husband and her son. When she got there, Ennode, her two-year-old son could not recognize her, as her face was sore and swollen. Afterward, they joined the Saint Gabriel community to go to the Central African Republic. They were afraid the war might get down to Bujumbura.

While Agnès was telling me the details of her Calvary, I begged her to stop. The details were too horrible to bear. However, with this testimony, I had a vague idea of how my parents and my sister had been killed. Concerning my brothers, Agnès told me they had dispersed, and she had no further news. After this harrowing first testimony, I went for a short siesta but could not stay quiet. Twenty minutes later, I left my room and went for a walk in the Bangui streets. On my way, I met people talking in my mother tongue and noted they were Rwandan nationals, particularly the officials of the Habyarimana government who had fled to Bangui. It was the first time in my country's history that the Hutus had fled massively to become refugees.

It was in Bangui also that I learned for the first time that priests and nuns had taken part in the crime of genocide. One day, together with my brother Alexandre and Brother Innocent, we went to visit to a group of nuns of the Sovu community in Rwanda who had fled to Bangui. I knew them, because I often used to go to their community for retreats with other young men aspiring to be Rogationists. When two of those nuns were accused of taking part in the genocide, I imagined that it was baseless slander. Honestly, I was unable to accept that the very nuns who used to get me into the atmosphere of prayer through hymns and psalms could participate in that horrible crime. Unfortunately, there was no slander. In 2001, Sister Consolata Mukangango, Mother Superior of the convent, and Sister Julienne Mukabutera Kizito were found guilty of the crime of genocide. They were sentenced respectively to fifteen and twelve years of imprisonment by a tribunal in Belgium, where they had found refuge after Bangui.

Some other religious people were reportedly involved. Father Athanase Seromba was accused of authorizing the destruction of his church in order to kill the Tutsis who had found refuge there. Pastor Elisaphan Hategekimana and his son Gérard Hategekimana, a doctor, were accused of taking part in the genocide at Mugonero, in Kibuye Prefecture. All this information was true, because they were found guilty of the crime of genocide and sentenced by the

International Criminal Tribunal for Rwanda in Arusha. With such cases, genocide was becoming increasingly difficult to understand. Before the genocide, all the criminals I knew had had a previous history of immoral living or were from circles known for bad conduct. But with the genocide, some priests, nuns, and pastors became executioners in horrific crimes. I could not understand what had happened with those women and men of God, as we used to call them.

Rwandan refugees in Bangui had very heartrending and troublesome testimonies. The two weeks I spent there, rather than relieving me, made me more psychologically vulnerable. I went back to Italy a bit depressed. The testimonies of my relatives and other Tutsis' Calvaries made me sick. They also took me back to my own route to Italy, where I landed seeking survival. At least, I still enjoyed the privilege of receiving comfort, even though I was unable to cope with the psychological suffering caused by the killing of my parents, brothers, and sisters. I do not know exactly whether it was the Bangui experience that induced me to change my status. But from my stay in Bangui on, I realized that I had to have my own family. I needed to love a woman so much, and to have children, even if I was aware that the project was going to take long to materialize.

Immediately after I arrived in Messina, I went to see Archbishop Ignazio Cannavò about this subject. After an attentive listening, it did not take this man of God long to understand me, and he pledged his support concerning my need to complete my studies. After a year in the Venturini community, I quit religious life once and for all and returned to normal civil life. For accommodation, the archbishop sent me to Galati St. Anna, in a guest house managed by Father Francesco Pati, a priest in the Diocese of Messina. I stayed there as a student in theology, and my only commitment was successful study. There were retired, elderly people in that house and a few younger people studying at secondary school. Father Francesco was a very good man. I used to stay at home, lonely, and he encouraged me to make friends and try to get out for relaxation.

Before I got used to this new situation, I often went to Jardini-Naxos in Di Pietro's family. As they had told me, the parents considered me their own son. With their children Carlos and Laura, I was at home, and they treated me as their own brother. In the family, everybody had his or her own car, and when I was there, I went out either with Laura and her friends, or with Carlos and his. Both were engaged. Laura's promised was Maximo, and Carlo's was Katia. Both were also friends to me. Sometimes, we all went to a restaurant at the Jardini-Naxos beach or we went to see their respective friends.

For feasts, we went to evening parties with a group of Laura's friends in a hotel belonging to Antonella's parents. Antonella was one of Laura's friends. She was always kind to me, and I was introduced to her mom, who was also informed that I had lost my parents. She was affectionate to me. Sometimes, she would pay my bill or give me presents. As a rule, the expenses of our evening parties were paid by Francesco Di Pietro, Laura's father. Before we went out, he would always give us money for our needs. He was very good, generous, and very compassionate to me. Before I went back to Galati where I lived, he would give me pocket money. He treated me as his own son. Unfortunately, he died in 2007, and I am sure God rewarded him for the good he did on Earth.

Matilde, Laura's mom, had sisters: Maria-Rosa and Elisa. Maria-Rosa had two children, Nino and Lidia, who were very sympathetic and affectionate. Elisa had also two children: Francesco and Alessandra. All these children treated me as if I were part of their extended family. Their families met often and invited me to spend happy moments with them. Laura and her friend Massimo had a group of friends. I can remember two sisters, Lucia and Maria-Rosa who used to invite us to play cards at their home in Taormina. I cannot forget Pina and Carmelina, who had put me through with Father Achille from Moio Alcantara. All these young ladies were always nice to me, and I was at home with them. On holidays or weekends, I was often with this group. Sometimes, they would take me to visit tourist sites in Taormina, or we would go eat pizza at this beautiful site on the seashore. They were all genuine friends and were happy to see me integrated into their group.

After those unforgettable moments with our friends, Laura and I would go back home late in her car. We respected each other, and her parents knew it. From time to time, she would introduce girls to me and wanted me to have my own girlfriend. But I could not engage in love relationships during that period. I was still under the authority of the Messina Archdiocese and found it better to wait until I was independent. But no one compelled me to that attitude. It was a matter of personal discipline. My friends often asked me questions on this subject, because they would not understand my position. Some even suspected I was a racist. One day, one of Laura's friends told me: "How come you haven't yet chosen your own girlfriend? Are you a racist, or has it anything to do with your culture?"

I was embarrassed by such words, but I knew perfectly well that I would get into trouble if I indulged in those relationships before I graduated. An African young man studying at the University of Lateran served as an example to me. He had a girlfriend and, without wishing it, she became pregnant. She had a baby, and the young student had no other option except to quit the university to take care of his companion and his baby. This unexpected change of status negatively impacted the young man's life. I did not want to get involved in a similar adventure. My studies came before everything else, and I was ready to sacrifice anything to complete them. I spared a few weekends and holidays for my friends, but on ordinary days I would go to St. Thomas Institute for classes and the library.

To go to there, I was rather lucky. I did not take the bus like most students. I used to go with Giovanni De Luca in his car. This young man lived near my boardinghouse and went to the same institute. He was in his second year of theology, like I was. He had been shocked by the horror that had befallen my country and had assured me of his support. He was always nice and close to me in my daily activities.

Father Francesco Pati, who was in charge of our house, was always good to me and had asked me to feel free to tell him whenever I needed something. For the two years I stayed at Galati, I had no problem with this priest who always encouraged me to get more familiar with the people of Galati.

Though I did not want to be a priest anymore, my faith and discipline did not change. I went to church each Sunday and prayed as usual. I often went to mass at Galati Marina Parish. The senior priest there was called Osa Agatino. He was also a friend of mine, and after my BA graduation in theology, he gave me support to further my studies in the social sciences in Rome.

I had many other friends in Galati who paid visits to me and supported me. They included a team of volunteers in the guest house, like Angelo and Mario from Mili Marina and Rosanna and Mariella from St. Stefano. All those people showed their friendship in one way or another. I particularly remember Angelo and Mario for inviting me to play on their volleyball team. Mili Marina had a volleyball team that practiced two days a week. I enjoyed playing with my team. Sometimes, we would play against other small teams in the area. The important thing was to play and socialize rather than win.

At St. Thomas Institute, besides Giovanni De Luca, who was often with me, most students in my class were friends of mine. Some showed their friendship more than others. I shall always remember Cesare Di Pietro, a student at Messina's major seminary. Before he was a student at the seminary, he had studied jurisprudence at Messina University. He was a serious and intelligent guy, popular with everybody. He was the kind of friend who was always close to me and cared, always asking if I had any problems. When I went to Rome to study the social sciences, Cesare was already a priest and doing his specialization at the Jesuit Gregorian University. We were not at the same university, but he had not forgotten me. He always cared and wished me a successful life.

At St. Thomas, most of the professors were Salesians, but there were a few others from religious communities in Messina. The Salesians were more demanding, and Don Fratallone was the one we feared most. He taught Ethics, and he was famous among students for failing the most people. To pass his exam, I had to work hard. Don La Piana Calogero was the best of the Salesians. He was also president of the institute. When I returned to Rwanda, I learned he had become archbishop of Messina. I was not surprised by this appointment. He deserved it, and I was very happy about it.

When I completed three years of theology, I obtained a degree but wanted to study the social sciences so much. I went to see Father Francesco Pati about it. Though I had to go to Rome to study, Father Francesco encouraged and supported me. I started collecting information on the universities that offered this program, and my friends recommended the Jesuit Gregorian University. I had also considered that, because I knew a few Rwandans who were studying there. The one remaining thing was go to Rome and get enough information regarding registration. The unconditional love suggested in the Bible was not a matter of theory for me. I was experiencing it constantly in Sicily.

In Sicily, Italy: with my volleyball team.
I am the black guy on the team.

In Sicily: with a group of friends. I am in the center.

CHAPTER 12

UNIVERSITY OF ST. THOMAS AQUINAS AND THE CENTER FOR EDUCATIONAL ORIENTATION

When I went to Rome to register with the Faculty of Social Sciences, I went straight to the Gregorian University Central Secretariat. Once there, I asked for the information I needed and was given the documents containing all the details, including fees and first-year admission requirements. After this, my intention was to take a train and return to Messina. When I got to the university gate, I met a Rwandan citizen I knew who was studying at that university. As we talked, he told me that not far from the Gregorian University was another university managed by the Dominican Fathers and was likely to be less expensive. I immediately went there for information to make a comparison.

When I was in the Central Secretariat of the University of St. Thomas, the dean of the Faculty of Social Sciences happened to be there as well. The secretary immediately told me: "You are lucky; here is the dean. He can explain better than I can." He introduced me, and the dean invited me to his office for more information. In the office, I showed him my philosophy and theology transcripts. I could see he was interested. Then, he gave me all the information on the academic unit. The information that interested me most concerned the possibility of finding a scholarship. He also recommended me to the manager of the Center for Educational Orientation (COE) for accommodations. With the beautiful words from Father Francesco Compagnoni, dean of the Faculty of Social Sciences, I made up my mind to register at that university.

The dean had just called the manager of the Center for Educational Orientation concerning my accommodations. He advised me to go immediately to his office at the Italian Episcopal Conference. I immediately left, happy and motivated. Once there, I introduced myself, and she did the same. Her name was Maria. She told me their center hosted other students from Africa, including students from the Cameroon, Nigeria, the Democratic Republic of the Congo, Angola, etc. At the end of our interview, I was morally stronger and felt God was still with me. I was going to leave Messina, the third major city of Sicily, for Rome, Italy's capital.

After the good news, I went back to Messina a very happy man and informed Father Francesco about my successful trip to Rome. He was also happy with those surprising events and drafted the recommendation documents for the COE. To end all this, he told me, I had behaved well in the community and that he would go on supporting my studies. With his encouraging words, I started saying good-bye to my friends, and, surprisingly, they all assured me of their support in case I ever found myself in trouble. More particularly, Father Tindaro from St. John the Baptist parish and Father Osa from Galati St. Anna parish shared the responsibility concerning the funding of my studies and accommodation in Rome. With all the support, I was moved and speechless. At five o'clock in the morning on the day of my departure, Angelo, the volunteer from our community, saw me to the Messina station in his car, and then I took the train to Rome.

I got to the Center for Educational Orientation in the afternoon. I was received by Cecilia, a volunteer at the center. She quickly showed me to my room on the third floor, where Father Oliver from Zambia and Father Antoine from the Cameroon also lived. There were other students, but they lived in a different house because they were not priests. These included Emmanuel from Liberia and Severino from Angola. There were also women: Bénédicte from Nigeria; Agatha from South Korea; and two sisters: Romaine from the DRC and Germaine from Uganda. Maria was manager of this Rome community, a branch of the Center for Educational Orientation with headquarters in Barzio, in the Lecco Province of Northern Italy. The founder of the center was a priest whose name was Francesco Pedretti.

Discipline at the center was required. Each day we would attend morning prayer followed by mass before going to the university. Before the evening meal, we would go to the vespers prayer. All the inmates had to abide by this timetable. Actually, the discipline was the same as in religious communities. But besides rigorous discipline, the COE was a very tidy place with a big garden. The accommodation fee was low compared to other houses in Rome. One day, a young Rwandan national living in Rome was informed that I was living in the center. He came to see me and asked what I had done to be admitted. He had interrupted his studies for work, being unable to pay for his accommodation as a student. Several times, he had unsuccessfully applied for a place at the center. Honestly, I knew what he had to do to gain admission: find a recommendation.

Yet, I also knew that if he were admitted, he would share my room. The young man was a Hutu, and tensions between the Hutus and the Tutsis were still hot at that time. It was a time when the destruction of Hutu refugee camps in DRC was in the headlines. As a Tutsi, I was aware that it would be a demanding test to live with a Hutu in the same room. So, when he asked for information on admission to COE, my answer was not straight. I took some time to think it over. Eventually, I remembered that I had decided to keep away from nurturing hatred, and I noted my constant progress thanks to heaven's intervention. Then, I made up my mind to show the young man what he needed to do to be admitted and become my roommate.

As a student at the University of Lateran, a church university, I was sure a recommendation from one of the officials at the university would do for admission to COE. I told him that I had been recommended by the dean of the Faculty of Social Sciences at St. Thomas University, and that he should fetch a recommendation from his dean. He did as suggested, and in a few days, he was sharing my room. He resumed his philosophy studies, and I had already taken care to avoid ethnic-based problems. These were common between the Hutus and the Tutsis then. With that resolution, I had no problem, though we did not agree on the Rwandan events. For example, he would not accept the idea that genocide had taken place in Rwanda in 1994. In his opinion, it was a war and nothing more. I avoided discussing this subject. I knew our views were so different. We lived in a multiracial community, and I had not seen any such problems. I was therefore convinced that it was possible for a Hutu and a Tutsi to live together in peace.

Beyond the Rome COE community, we were invited to participate in meetings in the Barzio COE community. Obviously, it was larger than the Rome community, and there were more people. The originality of the Barzio community was its multicultural educational program and the vast diversity of its members. They included young people from the Cameroon, the DRC, Bangladesh, Chile, etc. These young people stayed in the community for at least a year. But other young people came for shorter periods: from China, South Korea, Iraq, etc. It was impressive to see all those people from different countries praying and eating together every day, all without incident. I was happy to see that the young Rwandan living with me was also admiring that unity in diversity. When he graduated at the bachelor's level, he left the community to resume his job. He had met no problem with me.

When he left, I was the only Rwandan national left at the COE. But from time to time, I would invite other Rwandan young people studying in Rome to experience community life in the Barzio House. Besides Barzio and Rome, the COE had another house at Santa Caterina Valfurva in the mountains, a snowy place where people went skiing. During Christmas holidays, the COE would organize meetings and a program called *tutti in pista,* or "everybody on the track." We practiced skiing all morning. There were trainers for those who did not know how to do it. It was a great pleasure for me to play in the snow with people from all over the world. I had never seen snow in my country. In the afternoon, cultural meetings were organized, and each group tried to show the others something from its own country. Each time I went to those mountains, I went back to Rome with more energy and courage and was more focused on my work at the university.

Two years later at St. Thomas University, I had had no problem. I had made friends and was making good progress in my studies. But I did not know that my country's problems had gone beyond its own borders. When I arrived at that university, I found a young Congolese I had known when I was at Messina. We were happy to meet again, and he introduced me to his countrymen studying at St. Thomas. We were good friends until problems between our governments arose. Indeed, in 1998 conflicts were reported between Rwanda and the DRC. One day during the break, I joined my Congolese friend for our usual exchange. I noted that he was not willing to listen to me. I imagined he was not well and left. A few days later, I went to see him again, and he ran away from me. It was clear he did not want to talk to me, and I decided to leave him alone.

Another day, I was speaking with other students on the situation in my country. I uttered the name of Laurent Kabila, president of the DRC at that time. Even before I had finished my sentence, the Congolese guy, my former friend, raised his voice as he approached, proffering unbearable abuse. He was also gesticulating, as if he meant to hit me. With this nasty surprise, I was stunned, not knowing what to do. Another Congolese approached me in anger and was verbally aggressive to me. Fortunately, one of the other students decided to go and report to the dean of the faculty on the situation. Seeing the Congolese furious and aggressive, I left the classroom, and I saw the Dean coming in a hurry to see what had happened. He asked me to come back with him.

He was affected by that aggression. He had been informed about who the aggressors were. The dean delivered a difficult but constructive speech. On the whole, his speech was a straight warning to the aggressors that the culprit would be immediately sent away from the university if the incidents were repeated. He urged us to study harder instead of spending our time in useless quarrels. He ended his address by warning both Congolese that such attitudes were not tolerated at the university. After the speech, I felt relieved and more confident, but I knew I had to be careful in my movements. Problems remained outside the university. In 1998 in Rome, some groups of Congolese nationals were in league with Hutu extremists, and the Tutsis were not at peace.

During the same year, I made up my mind to go to Rwanda. I wanted to write my bachelor's dissertation on the situation of children, and needed data from the ground. When I informed the COE officials, their first move was to prevent me from going. I asked why they would not let me go to my country, and they would not respond. I kept insisting on an answer. Eventually, I was authorized, but saw they were keeping something from me. I went to Rwanda and did everything I had to do concerning my research. A month later, I was back in Rome.

When I was in the community with the other students, one of the officials from Barzio was there. He called me. I went to see him and sat down to listen. I was surprised that even before asking me how my trip had been, he asked a strange question: "*Quanti hai amazzati?*" or "How many did you kill?" I was appalled. A few minutes of reflection reminded me that Hutu extremists were intensively circulating false information on the situation in my country. To divert attention from the genocide they had committed, Hutu extremists were forging all kinds of lies. Sad, I told him: "If you ever discover that I killed someone while I was in Rwanda, take this rumor for truth. But if none were killed, why suspect me without evidence?" Rather than answer me, he sat thinking, a bit ashamed. I waited for his answer, and he asked me to change the subject.

This attitude from one of the officials at the COE was not a surprise to me. As said previously, it was due to a campaign of false information initiated by Hutu extremists and their friends against the victims of the genocide. The campaign was unfortunately going on in a number of European countries. Credulous people like this official fell into the trap without realizing it. Before our interview came to an end, I told him I had a project I wished to achieve with the assistance of the center. I proceeded, saying that it consisted of inviting young Rwandans of both ethnic groups to train on the multicultural activity taking place in their Barzio community. He was happy with my proposal, and he accepted on condition that I present the project to the whole COE community. A few days later, I presented the project in a meeting held at Barzio, and everybody was delighted.

The general objective of my project was to invite young Rwandan people of both ethnic groups to experience how people of different races and nationalities lived together in peace. Normally, the training lasted a year. After an experimental training of two young people, I planned to invite more young Rwandans to follow this program, which I found essential for the youth in a postconflict country like Rwanda. In my own way, I wanted to participate in the reconstruction of Rwandan society.

The COE officials had left me free to choose the two young people who were to come for the first round. As I was not in Rwanda, I entrusted a friend with the mission of finding two people who met the criteria I set with the COE. Two weeks later, my friend called to say he had found them and that they were willing to attempt the experience. I informed the COE officials without delay. They purchased the tickets and prepared other required documents. When they arrived at the Milan airport, I was already there to welcome them with a volunteer from the COE.

After getting out of the airport, we traveled to Barzio where they were well received by the whole community. I started explaining to them a number of things concerning community life at the center, and they showed they would find no difficulty adjusting. The only problem they gave me concerned their return to Rwanda after a year in Italy. They wanted to extend their stay in Europe. I immediately realized the young men would not return to Rwanda after training. I also noted that they were in contact with their friends in Belgium. They actually showed me that they wanted to leave Italy for Belgium, supposedly because they could not speak Italian.

With that attitude, I grew worried. I told myself that if they were successful in leaving for Belgium, I would be considered a crook by the COE. I then spent all my time convincing them to stay. Thank God! They renounced their project to go to Belgium, but they let me understand they would not return to Rwanda after a year of training. I could see they were not ready to understand my point of view: to find a solution together. Eventually, I asked them to at least talk with the COE officials.

With that lack of understanding, I realized my project had failed. As I had to go back to Rome for my studies, I left a disappointed man. However, I understood that my initiative to help and contribute to sustainable peace in my country could work against me. I was worried, and I tried to call the young people as often as possible to let them understand the importance of the training. I also asked them to talk sincerely and regularly to the COE officials about their desire to stay longer in Italy. Though I was still planning an application to the COE concerning training for other young Rwandans, I realized that everything depended on how the first round performed.

Concerning my studies, I concentrated on the preparation of my bachelor's dissertation. After graduation on this level, the possibility was open to go for a master's program. But after two years of higher learning in various Italian institutes and universities, I found it convenient to go back home and start working. I had resolved on this, though some of my Italian friends did not agree with my return to Rwanda, particularly in that period. When I told one of my professors about my resolution to go back home, he was amazed and discouraged me. He was convinced I would be sent to the front in the DRC as soon as I arrived in Rwanda. The propagation of false information on Rwanda continued, and I could see that my professor had a lot of pity for me. I was sure nobody was going to send me to fight in the DRC. I often called my friends in Rwanda and knew nobody had been obliged to become a soldier without his or her own consent. I had been used to all kinds of rumors ever since the 1994 Tutsi genocide.

During the month I spent in Rwanda in 1998, I had noted that everything negative reported about my country was incorrect. Rather, I had been surprised by the progress made in matters of peaceful coexistence between Hutu and Tutsi communities. The one thing that encouraged me most to return to Rwanda was the collaboration that existed between both enemy communities. Since the end of the genocide, the Government of National Unity had been created. The president of the republic was a Hutu, and the vice president was a Tutsi. The collaboration was also visible in all government organs. In the military area, some elements of the former Rwandan army had been merged with the new army. It was the first time in Rwanda that the Hutus and Tutsis joined to find solutions to their own problems. This positive progress urged me to return home a confident citizen.

Before going, I went to say good-bye to my friends in Sicily. When I told them I was going back to Rwanda, they all wished me good luck, and some of the most pious would invite me to pray together and ask God to assist me. I could not go back to Rwanda without seeing the two young Rwandans who were in Barzio. During our interview, I could still see signs of resistance concerning their return to Rwanda after their training. Given I would not be with them at that time, I advised them to tell the COE officials everything and to abstain from dangerous ventures on their own. Afterward, I said good-bye and returned to Rome to get ready for my trip home. At the end of their training, the two young people let me down and stayed in Italy where they are still working today. Following this, I was not courageous enough to renew my application with the COE to train other young Rwandans.

At St. Caterina, Italy: at a sports meeting organized by
the COE. I am on the left with a group of skiers.

CHAPTER 13

RETURN TO RWANDA: THE SILENCE OF NEIGHBORS

At the beginning of year 2000, I returned to my country after eight years in Italy. On the day I was to leave, Maria and Giuseppe saw me to Fiumicino Airport in their car, and I left for Kigali. Maria was in charge of the Rome COE House, and Giuseppe was a volunteer at the center. Once in the plane and perceiving clouds above us, I said silently: "Thank you, God; thank you, Sicily; thank you, Italy."

My brother Alexandre was waiting for me at Kigali International Airport. He lived in Butare, and we drove straight there. Previously, he had just spent two years home after a few years in France studying psychology. When he arrived in Rwanda, he was appointed manager of a center for the deaf-mute in Butare. With the aftermath of the genocide, his congregation had helped him buy a house where he collected all the survivors in my family. It was at Matyazo, a locality in Butare Town. My brother needed me to help in this family responsibility. When I got to the house, I found my younger brother Godefroid, my niece Francine, and another girl, Laetitia. There were two more young men, Innocent and Emmanuel. All five were orphaned by the genocide. Except for Godefroid and Francine, the other three had no remaining family.

First and foremost, I wanted to listen to their testimonies: what they had seen and experienced during the genocide. Godefroid, Emmanuel, and Innocent hadn't seen much. They had made up their minds to flee before the killings started. Godefroid was nineteen, the only person who had survived among my brothers and sisters who lived with my parents. Indeed, Theodore Sindikubwabo, interim president, had delivered an inflammatory speech that scared Godefroid to death. He made up his mind to flee immediately while the rest of my family were unable to decide. Like Godefroid, Innocent, and Emmanuel, young as they were, left just before the killings started.

Instead, Francine and Laetitia were only seven and experienced everything. They really survived by miracle, like Agnès. Francine had a heartrending testimony, only second to Agnès's. During the genocide, she lived with her family near my parents' home. Her father, François, was my eldest brother. According to her testimony, her father had already left when the killers arrived, convinced that men were targeted before women and children. But before the killers got to their house, her mother and the children had also run for their lives to the bush. While they were running, some children were separated from their mother. Francine remained with her, together with a two-year old younger sister strapped on her mother's back.

From where they were hiding in the bush, Francine and her mother witnessed how their familiar neighbors were transformed into looters: "They first looted our property, destroyed our house afterward, and took its building materials away," Francine said sadly. In the bush, they had nothing to eat or drink, and rain was abundant in that month of April. They spent a whole night in those hard conditions, and the baby was ceaselessly hollering. Realizing the killers were likely to uncover them anyway, Francine's mom decided to go back home with her children. When they arrived, they found their house a ruin with four walls only. The looters had taken away beams, tiles, doors, windows, etc. It was devastating and so sad. They remained in the ruins but had been spotted by the killers. They got them out of the ruins but decided against killing them on the spot and led them to the Akanyaru River instead. "The killers told us there were too many Tutsi corpses in the village and that it had been decided to throw women and children into the big river," Francine continued.

They gathered all the victims that had been snatched from their hiding places. They bound the hands of grownups, leaving children near their mothers. While the victims were being led to the river, their neighbors and the killers' children threw stones at them all the way, abusing them. All the people shouting were familiar to Francine, and none of them had pity on the innocent victims. The overwhelming feeling of the victims was that atrocious death was their fatality and that they had been forsaken by the whole world.

Francine remembered that some of the victims were stark naked, their arms bound, and were being beaten all along the way. When they arrived at the river, they met many other victims. They started killing adults before throwing them into the river. When it was Francine's turn, she was thrown into the river alive. Thank God! The killers were certain that the seven-year-old girl who did not know how to swim would not manage all alone. She told me, "I was thrown into the river and had no hope to survive. I first went deep into the water and then was brought back to the surface. Once there, I believed I was in heaven when I saw sunlight, because I had despaired of seeing sunlight again." Unconscious, Francine drifted downriver and eventually landed on the Burundi side of the riverbank. She woke up when she saw strangers helping her evacuate the water filling her belly. She was lucky, because a trader had been able to escape in time, and there he was. While Francine was drifting downriver, he was on the Burundi side of the river. When he saw the child was still moving, he paid some canoe men to retrieve her. Francine was unconscious when she was pulled out of the river and did not know where she was.

Afterward, she was taken to a Rwandan woman she used to know. She had been lucky enough to flee before the killings and was staying in a refugee camp with her three children. My brother Godefroid was also living in another refugee camp around and happened to learn about Francine. He came for her, and they spent a few days together in the camp before he found her a host family. It was a family of old Rwandan refugees who had fled in 1959. When the RPF army stopped the genocide, Francine returned home with that family. She will never forget that Godsend miracle.

As for Laetitia, her family were friends with mine. It was a big family of nine children. According to her, when the killings started, she ran away with her elder sister. The rest of the family also dispersed, each trying to find protection where it was possible. As a general rule, before they were killed, Tutsi girls were raped by their torturers. This is what happened to her sister. She was taken by a young Hutu who abused her while keeping her at his home for a few days. Realizing she had not been killed immediately, her sister begged the young man to keep Laetitia with them. He accepted, and they stayed together for about a month.

Unfortunately, the extremists informed everyone that the Hutus who were keeping Tutsi women in their houses were to hand them over to killers. Otherwise, they would be killed themselves. When the young man keeping Laetitia and her sister heard of the warning, he believed it to be groundless and kept the girls. But when the killers started searching houses and killing Tutsi girls who were kept by other Hutu young men, their protector hid them far from his home, believing nobody would know.

The killers knew the young man had the two sisters hidden somewhere. They threatened him and asked where he had hidden them. Laetitia could remember the young man coming toward their hiding place escorted by a group of killers. They all concentrated on her elder sister with bayonets and machetes, and no one was interested in the little girl who was petrified with terror. She wormed her way through the high grass and saved herself by the skin of her teeth. Realizing she could not stay alone in the bush, she hid in a thicket near the young protector's home.

When nobody could see her at night, she went back to the young boy and asked for protection. Thank God! He accepted Laetitia's request and hid her until the RPF army arrived in the region. But with their arrival, many Hutus fled to Burundi, and Laetitia's protector decided to leave. She begged him not to leave her by herself. He commiserated and decided to take her along. Once in Burundi refugee camps, the young man proceeded alone to Tanzania. With her protector's departure, Laetitia was in trouble, as there was nobody to take care of her. After a few days in panic and despair, a Tutsi woman married to a Hutu took charge of her in the camp, together with her own children, until they returned to Rwanda.

Francine and Laetitia's testimonies were so poignant that many scenes in their stories kept coming back to my mind for a few months. But they made my faith stronger still, as I continued to witness God's hand behind every survivor's miracle. I tried to explain my conviction to those children, and they had no difficulty understanding what I was saying. Since early childhood, they had been baptized in the Catholic Church and had remained devout Christians thanks to their family education. I came to realize their faith made it easier for them to understand that they were among the few privileged whose survival had been extraordinary.

I shared the responsibility for the protection and education of the children with my elder brother. Normally, they would stay at their boarding schools and would stay with me during the holidays. Orphaned children their age would often come to stay with them. It was beautiful to see the children play with their friends, in spite of their recent horrific experiences. Laetitia occasionally had trouble with her stomach, but otherwise they had no other difficulty at school or with their friends.

After the survivors' testimonies, I was eager to listen to our former Hutu neighbors' stories. They had seen everything. I had been informed that my family had not been killed by strangers or by people from afar but by some of our neighbors. With my brother Alexandre and two or three other people who would escort us, I went to the village where my parents used to live. Though safety was maintained all over Rwanda during the period, I would not dare go by myself to my village. We rode in my elder brother's community car, and when our former neighbors perceived the car, they hid in order to avoid our questions. Nobody wanted to look into our eyes.

Given the difficulty of talking to anyone in the village, we went to a commercial center where people would meet to drink banana wine. When they saw us, most of them went to hide, but Elias and Siméon, who were my father's friends, were courageous enough to come greet us. My brother started asking questions about who killed our family and where their bodies had been buried.

"We came here to learn the truth about who killed our family. Can you tell us what you know about it?" They lowered their heads, and no one answered.

"Let me repeat my question: can you tell us who killed our family at Kirarambogo? If you say nothing, I'll take you to the police station. There is no other way," my brother said.

"I really saw nothing. All I know is that your brother Antoine came to my house at night asking for a hiding place. I told him I couldn't hide him, as I was already hiding other people …" Elias confusedly said. He went on talking, emphasizing the fact that he had saved other Tutsi children. As for Siméon, he asserted that he had been sick all over the genocide period and could know nothing about it.

We came to understand that we would get no truth out of those people, and we made for Butare to wait for the opening of the gacaca popular courts. On our way back, we met Nkurikiye. His mother used to be a good friend to mine. We decided to stop and greet him. When we came to a stop, he made a move to go more quickly to avoid speaking to us, but I called to him.

"Nkurikiye, what's wrong with you? We're coming to greet you, and you run away. Don't you know us?" I asked.

"Oh, I hadn't recognized you," he answered lowering his head.

"Nkurikiye, you know our families were friends. We want to know the truth about the killing of our people," I said.

"I was very sick during that period and stayed at home," Nkurikiye declared. I took my time to explain there would be no legal proceedings if he told the truth, but he wouldn't change his mind.

Our neighbors had decided to hide what they had seen. We were disappointed and went back to Butare. The only hope for us was the beginning of the gacaca popular courts the government was organizing. On our way back, I started meditating on the forgiveness I had decided to give those who were responsible for killing my people after learning the truth. But I was confronted with the question of forgiving people who would not even show where they had thrown my family's bodies. Their attitude reactivated my confusion, and the anger that had subsided swelled up again. I talked to my brother about what we had just experienced. Seeing I was bitter and sad, he told me: "Remember, the extremists are happy when they see you so sad." His words awakened me to the realization that the struggle against the aftermath of the genocide was not a few days' business. Rather, it was a continual struggle and would perhaps last the rest of my life.

"In Rwanda: in front of our family house, which was destroyed during the 1994 genocide against the Tutsis."

CHAPTER 14

GETTING INTEGRATED INTO THE NEW SOCIETY

In July 2000, I signed a three-month contract with the National Program for Poverty Reduction after a few months of job searching. My work consisted in field data collection meant for the analysis of development indicators, like the population's education level, access to health care, household income, etc. With a team of investigators, I traveled up and down the former Butare, Kibungo, and Mutara Prefectures. Following an administrative reform, the former Butare Prefecture has presently become part of the Southern Province while the former Kibungo and Mutara Prefectures are both part of the Eastern Province. In my free time, I would talk to people about their problems resulting from the genocide. This way, at the end of the investigation work, I had more knowledge on the general image of my country's postgenocide society.

In 1998, I did some research for my bachelor's degree in social sciences, and I was overwhelmed by my discovery: the social fabric of Rwandan society in general had been rent, and this was especially true with regard to children and women. Various testimonies showed me that each Rwandan citizen had in one way or another directly experienced the genocide and its aftermath. No one was spared: one was either a genocide survivor, a refugee in neighboring countries, or a displaced person inside the country. Family and community had been previously fundamental in the lives of Rwandan people. The genocide had substantially changed that. Distrust was a reality among members of some families, and Rwandan society on the whole experienced ongoing suffering from the aftermath of the genocide.

The genocide unleashed widespread and systematic massacres. Even a number of Hutus killed members of their own families and considered them to be enemies if one of the parents happened to be a Tutsi. In Gisagara District, a young man named Karangwa was a genocide survivor. He publicly testified that he had fled his maternal uncle who had vowed to kill him. Karangwa declared that after his Tutsi father had been killed, his Hutu mother had decided to go back to her parents' to seek protection for her children. Once there, his grandmother did everything possible to protect her grandchildren. But their uncle would not bear the presence of those he called cockroaches in his place. He said they were Tutsis and had to die. With their uncle's threat, the children fled and managed to survive, thank God! Nowadays, Karangwa and his brothers openly accuse their uncle of his intention to kill them during the genocide.

In this case at least, the grandmother tried everything to save her grandchildren. In Kaduha, in the former Gikongoro Prefecture, it was quite the contrary. According to various accounts, one woman who had married a Tutsi decided to go back to her parents' to seek protection. Once there, her own mother would not hide her grandchildren, whom she considered potential enemies. Eventually, she came to the monstrous decision to kill them, and she did. Her daughter had already lost her husband. She was the victim of depression and in utter suffering. She died two years later. Other testimonies report similar cases in different villages all over Rwanda.

What I heard during my fieldwork in these regions was not different from what I already knew. It only confirmed that the aftermath of the genocide were rampant and the same all over Rwanda. I had been most affected by the problems faced by many households headed by women or children, or by those confronted by unaccompanied minors, such as street children. In my various interviews, I was made to understand that the genocide had especially taken the lives of men, leaving many widows and unaccompanied children. Also, many women had lost their husbands to police custody, because they had been accused of taking part in the genocide. These women lived alone with their children.

When my contract with the National Program for Poverty Reduction came to an end, I was personally interested in the issue of unaccompanied minors. According to different sources, many women heading households were confronting the heavy burden of accommodating unaccompanied minors. Massacres and displaced families all over Rwanda had left many lonely children who relied on themselves for survival: orphans, children who had been separated from their families during displacements, those who had left their families because of poverty, etc. This problem being so crucial, Rwandan families in general had the beautiful initiative to accommodate the children in their own households. After the genocide, very few families did not host such children.

In Butare, Martha is a widow whose husband was killed during the genocide. She remained with her four children and welcomed four orphaned sisters into her house at Taba. Dative had also lost her husband during the genocide. She raised three orphans together with her own children. Besides the cases of widows, a small number of men were widowers and lived alone with their children. Alexandre Karamage is a cousin of mine who lived in Kigali. When his wife and their only child were killed, he adopted Rwamucyo and Régine. Rwamucyo was his sister's only surviving child, and Régine was his elder brother's only surviving child. In addition to those two, he welcomed Chantal, his neighbor's little girl who was lonely after losing her entire family.

Concerning households with two living parents, notable generosity was also reported. The family of Déo and Béatrice lived in Kigali after the genocide and afterward moved to Butare. They accommodated six children orphaned by the genocide in addition to their own children. In Kigali, Augustin and Caritas raised their own children and added five children orphaned by the genocide. Vincent and Esperance, also in Kigali, had five children and adopted two genocide orphans. Usually, big families in Rwanda were common, but more so in the backcountry than in towns, because every family member had agricultural and/or livestock responsibilities. After the genocide, families living in towns were also obliged to accommodate orphans, very often in spite of their small incomes.

In spite of this generosity from Rwandan postgenocide families, many children lived alone in households headed by other children. According to various testimonies, the phenomenon existed almost all over Rwanda. I personally visited such a family in Matyazo, Butare Town, where over ten children lived in a small house. The head of this household was the oldest child, who managed to supervise the small ones. They all survived thanks to the generosity of a few individuals and, sometimes, the generosity of private or public organizations.

These families of children were happy enough to gather in households. They stayed together and managed to live in dignity. In some towns like Kigali, Butare, Gitarama, etc., some children lived in the streets. Some of these left their families because they were poor, because of family conflicts, or because both parents were dead. To survive in the street, some children would help carry things for people coming from the market, while others just lived by begging. To tackle this problem, the government created accommodation centers for those children, but some of them would not bear supervision in such centers. Quite often, they would end up in the street again. These were problems that were specific to women and children who had witnessed and experienced the genocide.

The old refugees also had their own problems. At the end of the genocide, Rwandan nationals who had lived as refugees in neighboring countries since 1959 returned home in great numbers. Their landed property before exile had been occupied by people who had stayed in the country. Once back home, some of the returnees were installed in parts of the Akagera National Park and in other unsettled areas. Others still could not easily find land of their own. Some people, especially in Kibungo Prefecture, shared their land with some of the returning refugees. On the one hand, this sharing deeds with former enemies left me with some hope, because it was a sign of peaceful coexistence between the Hutus and the Tutsis. But on the other hand, I imagined it would not last and that conflicts would erupt once again.

The aftermath of the war and the genocide did not affect human lives only; they also affected life in general. When in 2001 I arrived in Amayaga region, formerly in Butare Prefecture, I was stunned to see how far the environment had been damaged. Drought was endemic in this region and the sister Bugesera region. In the latter region, Lake Cyohoha and other lakes had considerably decreased in size, and a number of people had started fleeing the drought. Similar negative impacts of deforestation in other parts of Rwanda were a fact. This was true with Akagera National Park, Nyungwe and Gishwati forests, etc. It was also reported that the level of water in Lakes Burera and Ruhondo was low. Lake Ruhondo fed the Ntaruka hydroelectric plant in northern Rwanda, which supplied an important part of the country with electricity. Power shortages and cuts were common in Kigali City and big towns like Butare.

Witnessing such problems, I was afraid for the future of my country. I was often tempted to go back to Europe. But when I was about to make a final decision to leave Rwanda, I noted positive and encouraging signs. When I went to fetch my new identity card, I was surprised to see that there was no ethnic designation. Indeed, the policy of the government of National Unity had abolished the designation of ethnic groups in identity cards. Concerning access to education, all children who were able to go to school could do so. One day, a friend of mine told me how satisfied he was: "What I like with this government is that it gives all Rwandan citizens equal opportunities to education. My son had good grades and was given the possibility to choose his school. Nowadays, he goes at Ecole des Sciences de Byimana."

The effort of the new government was obvious in their determination to achieve national unity. After the genocide, Hutu infiltrators were fighting in Northern Rwanda because the genocidaires wanted to complete their genocide agenda. The infiltrators killed people while destroying infrastructure like administrative offices, health centers, and schools. The new government's attitude toward the infiltrators was amazing. Those who were caught during the fighting were reintegrated into the new army, and the youngest among them were sent to complete their secondary or university educations. A friend of mine was a genocide survivor and was in the army. He declared to me one day: "During our fighting, the infiltrators who are caught are integrated into the new army right away, and the youngest are sent to pursue their secondary or university education. I am afraid they will be our future leaders!"

While my friend found this reintegration a problem, it was a sign of hope to me. I saw therein a better future for my country. More encouraging still, the Commission for Unity and Reconciliation was created at the same time as the Commission for Human Rights. Vision 20/20 was already launched to fight against poverty. Seeing those positive signs of reconstruction, I made up my mind to become integrated into this new society and to stop thinking about going back to Europe. I started looking for some sustainable job, and after a few interviews, I was hired at Butare University Teaching Hospital where I worked as an administrative staff member and then as a social worker.

In their determination to get out of those post genocide problems, Rwandan citizens also devised another program, *Umuganda* or community work. It would take place once a month or whenever possible. It was focused on the maintenance of infrastructure like roads and schools, about anti-erosion work, afforestation on mountain slopes and wherever necessary. I was elected a member of the village committee whose duty included the organization of community work. After some time, I noted that on top of fighting against poverty, the community work also mended the fabric of Rwandan society in terms of reconciliation. All Rwandans—Hutus and Tutsis alike—organized these activities and worked together. After community work, people would gather in meetings where each village member exchanged opinions about their everyday problems.

Gradually, yet in quite a short time, signs of reconciliation between the Hutus and the Tutsis were visible. Very likely, this peaceful coexistence would also encourage reconciliation between Rwandan people and nature. Thanks to community work and other commitments of the Rwandan people, especially to afforestation, the Bugesera region, once an arid area, became the country's food basket. The level of water in our lakes and rivers rose, and Bugesera became also a tourist destination thanks to the birds there that can't be found anywhere else. The other country's tourist destinations started attracting more tourists than before, and new jobs were created gradually. With those signs full of promise in the reconstruction of my country, I still felt like I was bound to make my contribution, one that would be bear fruit.

CHAPTER 15

IN LOVE WITH A SURVIVOR OF GENOCIDE

I was looking for the woman of my life and uncovered another sick aspect of postgenocide Rwandan society. Many of the young people I met suffered from frustration, survivor's guilt, mistrust, and a lack of fulfillment. As a result of their parents or family members' participation in the genocide, a sizeable number of young people had unusual attitudes. Also, due to the miserable situation they had been through, some young survivors showed visible signs of trauma or strange behavior.

When I found a full-time job, I started looking for a girl to build a family with. To get there, I used my acquaintances, especially those I had before the genocide. I started going to families to build gradual and sustainable friendships. I was lucky to have a friend who was a famous psychiatrist. He often encountered people suffering from wounds of genocide. When I told him I was looking for a girl companion for life, he warned me: "Even before you consider marrying a Rwandan girl, please don't forget to ask her to go for an AIDS test. Many of the girls were raped, and many others have had unsafe sex in their many displacements." Many people in Rwanda often talked about this pandemic that added to the many problems already assailing postgenocide Rwandan society. I was really wary.

Even before making friends with any girls, I was acquainted with a young man who was single but planning marriage. We became good friends. One day, he asked me to go with him to see his betrothed. She lived with other young girls working in Kigali City. I gladly welcomed the invitation. It was a good opportunity to make new acquaintances of my own. My friend had a car, and we drove to the girls' home. We were warmly welcomed, and she introduced one of the girls staying with her. The latter girl was beautiful and charming, and she immediately kept my attention. While the two fiancés were busy talking, I concentrated on my new partner and noted her positive response. It was Saturday evening and I had an idea to invite the group for dinner and drinks. The idea had also occurred to my friend, and the ladies accepted when we made the suggestion. We went to a restaurant and ordered drinks and food. We wanted enough time with the girls. While we were waiting for the drinks, the fiancés were so busy talking to one another that I found a good opportunity to talk to that girl who was so fascinating to me. It was love at first sight.

As we talked, the girl gradually felt at home, and I was happy about it. She asked many questions to get to know me better, and I answered freely.

"I have no doubt you are a Catholic, as you went to university in Rome!" she told me.

"It's quite true; I am a Catholic, and I'll stay one. The Catholic Church has helped me so much in my life," I said.

"I used to be a Catholic before the genocide too, as well as my entire family. But when my parents and other family members were killed in the church they had found refuge in, I now have a kind of phobia and cannot enter a Catholic church. I am presently a Protestant, a member of a new church," she declared. I was overcome by pity and frustration by her declaration, but I made no comment.

When she noted that I was affected by her words, she was encouraged and invited me to her new church for prayer the next day. I thought it over for a moment, and I accepted her invitation. The other two were following our conversation but pretended otherwise. It was already late when we finished our meal, and we drove the ladies home. We too went home, and my friend immediately encouraged me to push on with the girl. I agreed but was internally feeling uneasy about a girlfriend who would not enter a Catholic church.

The next day, I rose very early to get ready to see my friend to prayer. Honestly, it was my first time going to prayer in a church other than a Catholic church. I had to go and fetch her from home, as she had asked. She was happy when she saw me, and we left for her new church where a congregation had already gathered. I was expecting to see a church similar to the Catholic churches. To my surprise, the prayer house was a kind of shed under construction, quite unlike the prayer houses I used to know. The prayer style was very different and very long. At the time, I was uneasy and wanted to leave before the end of the prayer meeting, but I persevered. I did not want to offend my new friend.

After three hours of prayer, we left, and she asked how I had found her church. I politely told her that the prayer had worn me out, and that I would not come back. Straightaway, she said that the first thing I was to do was leave the Catholic Church and get baptized into her church if I wanted to be her friend. I realized I could not go ahead with her but said I was going to think it over.

"Think it over properly. I'll be waiting for you in our church next week," she kindly responded. Honestly, I was unable to come back to the church and did not know what to do about the girl.

When I next met my friend's fiancée, she confirmed the girl had pledged to marry only a member of her church. However, she added that she liked me and was waiting for my conversion. My friend's fiancée was happy that her girlfriend kept thinking about me and encouraged me to convert if I wanted a total conquest. I thought it over but came to the conclusion to continue with the Catholic faith that had given me so much. On the following Sunday, I did not go to my friend's church as I had been asked. It was the end of our short-lived friendship.

After this short experience, I went back to Butare, and on my way I kept musing about that charming young lady who was unable to go back to a Catholic church because of the genocide. No sooner had I returned home than my friend's fiancée called me. I could sense sadness in her voice.

"How can you be so malicious? You never told me that your friend, my fiancé, was a Hutu! It's all over! I cannot live with a Hutu. My greatest misery is that you knew about it and you didn't tell!" I was a bit annoyed but used a firm and convincing tone.

"Well, when I got acquainted with your fiancé, he lived alone with his Tutsi mother. He told me he had never known his father who died when he was only six months old. Besides, I know your love is faultless so far. Honestly, I don't understand how you can make a decision like this one, even if he is a Hutu," I said.

"You are malicious, you are so malicious ..." she said and hung up.

I was overwhelmed by this affair. The girl was already four months pregnant from her fiancé. When I called him, he was sad but assured me he was going to talk to her to know what exactly had happened. Usually, before she gets married, a Rwandan young girl's family must inquire about the suitor's ethnic group. She must have a go-ahead from her family in order to marry him. In my friend's case, the girl's family had inquired and found out that he was a Hutu. They opposed the union.

Even if the new government had abolished the designation of ethnic groups in Rwandan citizens' identity cards, anyone wishing to know someone's ethnic group could know it. Where my friend was concerned, his father's name was on his identity card as always, and this was an easy way to identify the son. Before the genocide against the Tutsis, the young man was proud to be called a Hutu and his mother happy to have a Hutu husband. But after the genocide, he built on his father's death and rejected his Hutu identity. To convince people of his Tutsi identity, he said that his mom had been unfaithful and had an affair with a Tutsi, her son's real father. The presumed Tutsi father had died during the genocide. Nobody knew whether the declaration was true or not. But according to their neighbors' testimonies, the mother confirmed that his father had been a Tutsi.

To win his fiancée back, the young man told her this story and asserted he was a Tutsi. Eventually, they got married, had children, and are still living together. After this experience, I learned and witnessed other stories of young people who were frustrated and suffering from a guilt complex due to their relatives' responsibility in the genocide. I knew that such wounds would take long to heal.

In a situation like this one, I trusted God would help find a woman. Every evening after work, I would go to mass and prayer at St. Thérèse's Church in Taba, Butare. Emmanuel Twagirayezu, the senior priest at Butare Parish at that time saw me every day at mass. One day, he told me: "Hormisdas, if you still feel like becoming a priest, feel free to let me know." He imagined I had a calling for priesthood while I was praying for a girl to marry. I went on praying every day and trusted that one day, God would answer my prayers.

One Saturday, I went to a friend's wedding ceremony in Butare. After mass, we joined the reception hall, and I sat far behind, where I could still manage to find a place. While I was looking around for a familiar face, a young lady who was looking for a seat arrived and sat next to me. I looked at her and thought she looked nice. I started talking to her and politely asked her name. She was Marie-Claire. She was reserved at first but gradually became more at home with me and even more beautiful. Before we parted, I wanted to ask for her address, but something held me back, and I left without it. Afterward, I regretted not even asking for her telephone number. It was too late.

My duties at the university teaching hospital included preparing meetings of the institution's board of directors. One day, I needed a document that was necessary for the board. I went to look for it in the hospital administrator's office and was surprised to find Marie-Claire there. She was happy and got up to say hello. I gave her a warm hug. She was there to submit her file for a nurse's job. The administrator was examining the file and declared he was happy to have a nurse with a bachelor of science degree. This category of nurse was rare at the hospital. The administrator gave me the document I needed along with Marie-Claire's file, which was to be presented before the board. Before leaving the hospital, she came by my office for more information. I took the opportunity to ask for her phone number. A few days later, Marie-Claire came for the written exam and the interview. She was selected.

Since the moment I won her telephone number, I called every day, and we were often together. Even before starting her work at the hospital, Marie-Claire had become my best friend. When she started, we met every evening, and we have never parted since. One day, Marie-Claire told me how she had survived by the breadth of a hair. She was fourteen then, in her first year at middle school. When militiamen came to their home, she was with her family. Before killing her mother and elder sister, they took her father away from the home and killed him, and then came back for them. They killed her mother in front of her and hacked her sister with a machete. She did not die straightaway. After killing the grownups, the militiamen looted their house and took everything away, leaving Marie-Claire and her nieces, Aline and Nadège, alive. Aline and Nadège were still very young. They went in hiding in the banana grove next to the house from where Marie-Claire could hear her elder sister's moaning. This moaning would often come back to her until the day she told me the horrible story.

Together with the other children, they left not knowing where to go. Eventually, Marie-Claire and her nieces got to her maternal aunt, who had married a Hutu. They hid there until the end of the genocide. Thank God! She had an elder sister Beatrice who lived in Burundi. She was married to Déo, and when they returned home after the genocide, they learned about Marie-Claire and her nieces. They fetched them and lived together. My future wife's story affected me and my love for her grew even greater. Marie-Claire lived in Beatrice's family together with many other orphaned children: her nieces Aline and Nadège; Deo's nephew, Désiré; and Jean-Marie and Jeanne. According to Marie-Claire, they were a really generous family. Other orphaned children would spend a year or more with them before finding another welcoming host. Their house was a home for children orphaned by the genocide.

Concerning our friendship, I had no worry with Marie-Claire, and I was certain I had hit my target. A few months later, we decided to marry. The only likely difference was our religious identity. She was a Protestant in the Anglican Church, and I was a Catholic. I asked her to keep her faith and she refused, offering to be received in the Catholic Church. This was done at Butare Cathedral. The following month, we started getting ready for marriage, which took place at St. Thérèse in Butare.

Francine and Laetitia already lived with me, and we kept them after our marriage. A few months later, we also accommodated a young girl going to a secondary school in Butare. She had nowhere to live. Her father was in prison, guilty of taking part in the genocide, and her mother was unable to pay her school fees. We were not related at all. We just wanted to help someone who was different, someone who needed our assistance.

We knew perfectly well that her father was in prison when we welcomed her, but she would not acknowledge him as her father. She would say her father was someone else. But we were used to this type of frustration and guilt complex with young people with family members who were responsible for the genocide. Except for those frustrations, she had no problem with us. She stayed until she completed secondary school.

The frustration and guilt complexes found with such young people in Rwanda have inspired artist Edouard Bamporiki Uwayo. He wrote a book in Kinyarwanda, *Icyaha kuri bo, ikimwaro kuri jye: igiti mwateye, dushaririwe n'imbuto cyeze* or *Their Sin, Our Shame: The Sour Fruits of the Tree You Planted.* After the publication of his book, the artist created an association, Arts for Peace to help those young people to heal from these wounds. Through talking and helping them to tell the truth, some have started their healing process thanks to the association. But the truth is always difficult to tell. We are going to see this in the next chapter about the gacaca popular courts.

In Rwanda: me and my wife Marie-Claire on our wedding-day.

My family, a year after marriage. From left to right: Francine,
me, Laetitia, and my eldest daughter, Davina.

My family today. On the left, I'm holding my little
daughter, Anaïs; in the center, my eldest daughter,
Davina; and on the right, my wife, Marie-Claire.

CHAPTER 16

GACACA POPULAR COURTS

After the genocide, the new government decided it was good to refer to Rwandan culture, to find a solution to the many problems that assailed Rwandan society. The gacaca courts were created within this framework. I impatiently waited for the gacaca courts to begin. I wanted to know the truth about the murder of my family. *Gacaca* is a Kinyarwanda word for "soft lawn," traditionally a place where people would meet to settle disputes among neighbors or families in a village. It was an assembly of village people chaired by people of integrity and where everybody could speak. The gacaca courts aimed the eradication of the culture of impunity that had prevailed in Rwanda since 1959, the recovery of truth on the genocide events, the promotion of reconciliation, and the rehabilitation of social coexistence.

Since I had returned to Rwanda, I had wanted to discover who had killed my family and where their bodies had been thrown. Of the eight people killed in my family, only my parents' bodies had been found. The other six, brothers and sisters, could not be found, because my neighbors wouldn't tell. To contribute to the reconciliation between Hutus and Tutsis, I had decided I would forgive those who were responsible for my family's death if I could know the truth and bury them decently. I only needed someone to confess responsibility.

When the gacaca courts started, I was working at the Butare University Teaching Hospital. Every Wednesday afternoon, we were allowed to go and take part in the proceedings of those courts. I lived in Taba and would go to the courts in that locality. But my plan was also to participate in my native village courts, when it was time to examine my family's files. In Taba, a short period of information gathering was first initiated. Every person who lived there during the genocide was asked to provide information on the events experienced and witnessed.

On the first day of gacaca courts, I went to the gathering held at Ecole Autonome de Butare in Taba. The leader of the gathering addressed the assembly, explaining the phases of the gacaca courts in that village. He had a secretary who was in charge of recording the testimonies of people who had lived there during the genocide. To start with, a young man spoke, directly addressing a young woman who worked at the National University of Rwanda. He asserted that he had seen her with a militia that had kept the town of Butare in terror. He did not pretend that he had seen her kill anybody. He just asked what she had been doing in such a group.

Embarrassed and confounded, the young girl, instead of reporting what she had seen, defended herself relentlessly, denying everything the young man had said. She was not the only person to be addressed. A gentleman who taught at the National University of Rwanda when the courts were in session had been seen in that militia during the genocide, and he was asked to say what he had seen. Rather than reporting, he proceeded to defend himself, accusing the whole gathering: "As you can see, I am a university lecturer, and you just want to throw me into prison ..." The gathering leader tried to calm them down, reminding them that it was time to report what each had seen, and that the trial had not yet started. In turn, other people reported their experiences, but the two who had been singled out did not. They kept defending themselves. After two sessions, they would not come back, and I came to learn that they had left Rwanda even before the gacaca courts got to the trial phase.

In 2005, the phenomenon of fleeing the country was widespread for people suspected of taking part in the genocide. In Gisagara District, such people fled massively to Burundi, and the Rwandan government had to send a mission to mobilize them. Many returned, but many others did not. A rumor was going around that the Rwandan government had purchased a machine that was to grind all the Hutu.

Those departures did not stop the gacaca meetings. In Taba, we used to meet every Wednesday to listen to testimonies. There were very few genocide survivors, but our group was lucky enough to have some: Athanase had hidden in the ceiling of the restaurant where he worked; Margarita was a widow who had lost her husband and seven children. She had seen and heard almost everything in Butare Town, because she had changed hiding places before she eventually settled at the University Teaching Hospital. The testimonies of both survivors agreed on many facts. For example, they informed the gathering that Professor Karenzi, a lecturer at the National University of Rwanda, was first to be killed in Butare. It happened on the main avenue in front of Hotel Faucon, for all to see. Heartrending testimonies proceeded, each detailing what had been seen or heard.

One day, the gacaca court in Taba invited a priest who used to manage the Institut Catéchétique Africain to testify. Some survivors had seen him at a road checkpoint set in front of the Institute, and he was asked to say what he had been doing there. He did not deny his presence at the checkpoint but asserted he regularly went there to protect his institution. Road checkpoints had become famous slaughtering grounds during the genocide, and someone asked him if anyone had been killed at that particular checkpoint. "Oh, a young man was uncovered from his hiding place and killed at our checkpoint," the priest declared. Concerning the question whether they had weapons, he asserted there was only one gun. When the trials began, the priest was found guilty and sentenced to nineteen years imprisonment.

The trials were held in Butare Multipurpose Hall. Butare University Teaching Hospital was one of the most well-known hiding places in the town. Some of the Tutsis who had hidden there had survived and testified. A nun who was in charge of the cooking at the hospital was accused of taking an active part in the genocide. The survivors also accused a doctor who worked in the department of gynecology. The nun and the doctor were eventually found guilty and sent to prison. There were other presumed genocidaires: one Protestant pastor, one police officer, the chief of Butare's police force, as well as some military officers and soldiers, secondary school teachers, peasants, etc.

Besides genocide survivors, critical eyewitnesses were found among the prisoners who had pleaded guilty and who had decided to tell the truth and actively participate in Rwandan reconciliation. After confession, their sentences were reduced, and by 2008, many of the repentant prisoners had been set free. I was hoping that with the repentant people in Kirarambogo, I would be able to learn the truth about the killing of our parents, brothers, and sisters. I was informed that Jonas, one repentant man from our village, was going to say everything about it. Jonas was one of the killers' leaders at Kirarambogo. He had confessed to killing a few people. But concerning my family members, he confessed he had only slapped my nephew Ennode's face before the genocide, and he now looked to him for forgiveness. But even before the gacaca courts started,

Agnès, my elder brother's wife, had told me about my sister Marthe's experience before she was killed. She had said that Jonas had sought her from her hiding place. Moreover, before she was thrown into Akanyaru River and survived, Agnès had seen Jonas leading killers. But because Jonas had confessed to killing a few people and because there were not enough testimonies to charge him with my sister's death, he was set free.

Another repentant person was Maniraguha. He confessed to being with the group of killers who had killed my parents. My father and mother had gone hiding at Claver's, a neighboring Hutu's home where killers found them. When they arrived, they asked Claver to throw my parents out. He hesitated, and the killers started breaking his house doors and windows. Realizing they would be uncovered anyway, my parents went out, and the group of killers took them near our home and killed them. Their bodies were left unburied, in the open. When my brother Godefroid went back to our former home a few months after the genocide, they were still there. Like Maniraguha, Mpitabakana also confessed to being in the group that killed my parents. In spite of all the confessions, nobody accepted responsibility for killing my six brothers and sisters, and none said where their bodies had been thrown.

Whoever followed the gacaca sessions in Kirarambogo noted that the supposedly repentant people sought the reduction of their sentences above all else, including the truth about the genocide. In reality, there had been very few Tutsis in our village. They lived among their Hutu neighbors, and there were no separate sections reserved for Tutsis or Hutus. The innocent people were not killed by people from elsewhere. Jonas, who had confessed to taking part in the genocide, used to teach at the same primary school as my sister Marthe. Maniraguha was an ordinary peasant. Given this situation, I was unable to know how my brothers and sisters had been killed.

Supposedly, nobody knew who had killed them and where their bodies had been thrown.

Gacaca courts in Kirarambogo had their peculiarities: there were few survivors, and almost all the judges and witnesses were Hutus. Therefore, they did everything to reduce the number of condemnations, as the accused were often members of their families or their neighbors. Concerning the death of my younger brother Michel, one courageous woman said everything, accusing the man she considered to be responsible for the youth's death. Unfortunately, her testimony was not validated, as no other testimony came to support her accusation.

Like this woman, my sister-in-law Agnès, was aware that her testimony would not be validated, but she decided to tell the whole truth about what she had witnessed. In her testimony, she cited the names of her neighbors who had taken part in her Calvary before throwing her into Akanyaru River. They knew perfectly well that Agnès was the unique survivor in her group and that her only testimony would not be sufficient to condemn them. So, they categorically denied their role. But a few days later, three among them fled to Burundi. They spent a few months there and then came back home. Every time they met her, they would change direction, because of shame. In spite of these worries, Agnès finds her survival more important than her former executioners' attitude of denial, and I am very happy about it. She is constantly grateful to God. This attitude urges her to tolerate the viciousness of these men, and she is now free of hate.

Christine was a young girl going to secondary school before the genocide. She lived with her family at Kirarambogo. When the killings of the Tutsi started, she found a hiding place at Martin's, a young teacher who accepted to protect throughout the three months of genocide. From her hiding place, she used to ask for news of her family, and Martin told her everything. When her father was killed, Martin gave her the names of the whole group who sought him out from hiding as well as the name of the person who killed him with a spear. After her father's death, she also learned that all her family had been killed. She had nothing to do and was not sure she was going to survive. At the end of the genocide, she often met her father's killer as well as the leader of the group that had sought him out.

When the gacaca courts started, Christine accused Gaspard. He had led the group that had taken part in her father's death, as well as Karake, who had finished him off with a spear. She was lucky enough to have Martin, Thérèse, and another person for support witnesses. In spite of all this, the judges in that court did not find the accused genocidaires guilty. Christine was sure of their crime. She was not discouraged and asked that those people be referred to another gacaca court. The second gacaca court was also partial, and Christine was disappointed. Eventually, they were referred to a third gacaca court that found them guilty.

Another survivor was Rutayisire, the son of Kanyamiryango. He had fled before the killings started in Kirarambogo. After the genocide, he returned to his family's home and found nobody. Everybody had been killed. Without delay, he asked his close neighbors what had happened. Two brothers, Joseph and Jean, as well as their mother, asserted that his father and some other family members had been thrown into the Akanyaru River. Rutayisire trusted their declaration and prepared to survive alone. Toward the end of the gacaca courts, he was working in his farm one day when he found a hole where someone's body had been thrown. Using the clothes around the body and some other signs, he was able to identify his father's body. He was shocked, called all his neighbors, and told them about the two brothers and their mother's declaration. Before the evidence, everybody was speechless, including the liars.

As Rutayisire was afraid his village court was going to be partial, he asked that the three of them be referred to another court, which found them guilty.

It was difficult to find the truth about the genocide in Kirarambogo. I started to wonder how I was going to forgive people who would not participate in the reconciliation process. Besides the indifference, provocations were common. One day, a genocide widow asked me how one could forgive people who went on using vicious words to the victims. She told me that when a repentant prisoner was released after fifteen years in prison, his wife came to her and said: "My husband is back home, enjoying life with his entire family. When is yours coming back?"

Listening to such testimony aroused the anger and anguish I had stifled. Our neighbors' viciousness revived my suffering and brought me back to the early days of the genocide. But my decision to forgive and to remove these torments was stronger than the provocations. But still, I was wondering how I was going to forgive someone who did not confess. Even the two people who had confessed their participation in my parents' death only did so before the court to get free. They never asked us for forgiveness.

This experiment made me envy the survivors who had been lucky enough to find guilty people who were ready to seek forgiveness. Immaculée Ilibagiza, author of *Left to Tell*, is a survivor who forgave her relatives' killers. Reading her story, I told myself: "How lucky she is!" Jean-Paul Samputu, another survivor, had forgiven a killer who had sincerely confessed. When I listened to his testimonies, I asked myself: "Why won't such things happen to me?" In Mushaka, Western Province, former enemy families were working together in friendship, thanks to seeking and giving forgiveness, according to the Bible. Touching examples in this category abound in this parish. But these values are highest in their role of channeling intense social links when a young man marries the daughter of his father's killer, an event that took place in Mushaka. With the assistance of Father Ubald Rugirangoga, many Catholics in Mushaka Parish sought and offered forgiveness and achieved sincere reconciliation. From 2009 to 2013, 117 former genocidaires and victims' families have been reconciled.

With these examples of reconciled people, I still hope that one day, sincere forgiveness seeking and receiving shall take place in Kirarambogo. I remain convinced that my modest contribution in the area of reconciliation shall bear fruit. But as my neighbors had robbed me of the opportunity to forgive them, I opted for my own strategy. I decided to write a book and show that constant gratitude toward my creator would not allow me to nurse hatred. Rather, it leads me to unconditional love that may reach my family's killers, in spite of their refusal to collaborate. Let these people know that I forgive them, hoping that one day they shall overcome the obstacles and shall lay down their burdens by telling the truth about their deeds. I am aware that our human nature has limits. It is the reason why I always seek a solution to my suffering in God's word in the Bible, the world's most read book and bestseller. I opted for realism while seeking the assistance of heaven, the assistance of God, creator of all men. To come back to my family's death, I am writing another book to show the killers, through concrete examples, that truth is essential for them. It is not the will of God that these Rwandan citizens die spiritually. The will of God is that they convert and live in peace with themselves, with all Rwandans, and with the whole world.

EPILOGUE

GRATITUDE RATHER THAN HATRED

I was in Rome one day, telling my story to a friend who was a refugee there. I was talking about how the many blessings I had received from God deserved high recognition. He immediately answered with emphasis that my gratitude was motivated by the fact that the Tutsis had recovered the power they had lost in 1959. He also took the opportunity to show his discouragement and despair. He was a Hutu and regretted the Hutu leaders' failure. When I tried to explain why he too owed some gratitude to God, I noted my words bored him. He kept saying that I was boasting, because the Tutsi Rwandan Patriotic Front had been victorious over Hutu power. I tried my best to explain but to no avail. Our exchange ended without compromise.

After this exchange, I wanted to know what some young Tutsis studying in Rome were thinking. I organized, met, and discussed with each. By the end of my modest research, I had come to understand that most of those youths found me to be a naïve person. Some of them kept asking: "How can you dare speak of gratitude when you have lost almost all of your family?" I finally realized that my discourse on gratitude only three years after the genocide remained unintelligible to them. But given the genocide and its aftermath, my opinion was that every Rwandan still living should be aware of the favors received to understand the importance of gratitude.

Traditionally in Rwanda, one who received a cow as a gift from a friend was bound to return a heifer descending from the cow to the giver. It was performed in an official ceremony before guests, friends, and acquaintances, the gift of a cow in Rwandan culture being the highest in value. Normally, tradition wanted the receiver to praise his sponsor in public as often as possible. The practice was known as *Kwirahira uwaguhaye inka* in Kinyarwanda.

This practice still exists today and has improved considerably. The *Girinka munyarwanda* program, or "a cow for each Rwandan" consists in giving a cow to one who has none in a bid to eradicate poverty. In turn, the receiver, rather than returning a heifer to the giver, would give one to the neighbor who has none, following the giver's recommendation. Each new receiver would continue the chain until each poor Rwandan citizen had a cow.

The gift of a cow is highly valuable for Rwandans, but the gift of life is still more important. Rwandans of all creeds know that a newborn child is a gift of God, and this is expressed in Rwandan names: *Muhawenimana*, or "given by God" and *Habyarimana*, or "only God has children." When somebody is successful or recovers from a serious decease, Rwandans usually say that God was there to help, *yagize Imana*, to mean literally "he/she was with God" or "he/she was lucky." For Christians, when somebody dies, we say: *Imana yamuhamagaye*, or "God called him/her," and during burial ceremonies we ask God to give the deceased eternal rest: *Imana imuhe iruhuko ridashira*. Actually, Rwandans constantly appeal to God in their everyday lives.

As a general rule, the value of gratitude was trampled and ingratitude promoted during the genocide. To get to the genocide, Hutu extremists had first of all elaborated and adopted what they called the Ten Hutu Commands. They were the opposite of God's commandments. Without these hate commands that took the majority of Rwandans away from their origin, the genocide might not have been possible. According to various sources, those Ten Hutu Commands were used for the first time in 1959. Then, they were followed by widespread persecutions of the Tutsis. In 1990, *Kangura Daily* recuperated and revived them, adapting them to the new situation. And the killings of the Tutsis followed relentlessly until the 1994 genocide.

Our elites of the first two republics ungratefully used the blessings received in their lives to destroy other people's lives. These include education and economic power. Through the practice of the negative value of ingratitude, the extremists did not achieve much, though. On the contrary, they are presently paying a heavy price for their actions. They are either in prison or wanted by national and international courts. In any case, no genocide perpetrator is living in peace. There are many examples of such people. The following paragraphs describe some of those who were tried by the International Criminal Tribunal for Rwanda in Arusha or by other courts.

Jean Kambanda, prime minister of the interim government, comes from Southern Province in Rwanda, like me. When I saw his handcuffed picture before the International Criminal Tribunal on television, I understood the meaning of the saying that hatred shall beget hatred. During the genocide, Kambanda used to sensitize the population to active participation in the crime. When his government was defeated, he fled and was wanted by the Arusha International Criminal Tribunal. He eventually confessed, was found guilty, and was sentenced by that tribunal to life imprisonment.

In my Muganza Sector in Southern Province, Callixte Kalimanzira was the most educated and respected man, a role model for the youth who dreamed of success in life. He had been an elementary school classmate of my elder brother François. He had then gone to secondary school at Groupe Scolaire de Butare, one of the best schools in my country, and later studied at the National University of Rwanda and graduated as an agricultural engineer. In 1982, he started work as director of agricultural projects. Afterward, he worked as subprefect in Butare Prefecture. During the genocide, he was already a cabinet director in the Ministry of Home Affairs.

During the genocide, he became famous for supervising killers, especially on Kabuye Hill, where many terrorized Tutsis had been gathered. After the horror of the genocide, he fled Rwanda for Kenya. He knew he was wanted and made up his mind to turn himself in to the Arusha International Criminal Court. When he was fifty-four years old, he was sentenced to thirty years in jail for the crime of genocide.

Still in the Southern Province, a woman had become famous as a genocidaire and was later prosecuted for sensitizing killers to rape their victims before killing them. Her name is Pauline Nyiramasuhuko. She was no ordinary woman. She was the minister of family and women's promotion. Maurice Ntahobari, her husband, was rector of the National University of Rwanda. I used to know them in Butare. They represented the ideal, successful married couple. At the end of the genocide, Pauline fled but was eventually taken to the Arusha International Criminal Court for Rwanda, together with her son Shalom Ntahobari, who was a leader of killers and rapists in Butare. The mother and her son were found guilty and sentenced to life imprisonment.

A father and his son are respectively a pastor and a doctor, from Western Province, formerly Kibuye Prefecture. Pastor Elizaphan Ntakirutimana and Dr. Gérard Ntakirutimana took part in the genocide at Mugonero and were prosecuted for that. Usually, a pastor is considered a healer of souls and a doctor a healer of the body. Those two unfortunately opted to become genocidaires. Eventually, they were successfully tracked by the international justice authority and were prosecuted and sentenced: the father to ten years in jail and his son to twenty-five.

Compared to the victims of the genocide, including our parents, brothers, sisters, and neighbors, every living Rwandan today should consider himself or herself privileged. Some modesty will suffice to remind us how invaluable this gift of life is. A million Rwandans were not lucky enough to go on living even though they wished to. Rather, they were atrociously killed, totally deserted. And I firmly believe that some Rwandans today were saved by miracles and that God's kindness is highest in the peaceful cohabitation among genocide survivors and their former victimizers.

From my viewpoint, these extraordinary facts in post-genocide Rwandan society are not the product of Rwandans' determination alone. They are also miracles God ceaselessly performs for our country. I have never heard of any such case anywhere else in the world. All Rwandans should therefore recognize the extraordinary aspect of these blessings and always practice gratitude toward God.

My name symbol is a heritage from my father and his gratitude and faith in God. These values have had an efficient healing effect on my wounds from discrimination and the genocide. The good I experienced through them is my only wealth. I wish to share this wealth with Rwandans, in particular, and, in general, with every human who was in one way or another wounded and seeking full and sustainable peace.

For certain, the constant practice of gratitude toward God urges me to unconditional love. I feel always ready for any sacrifice to have my family's killers converted. I know that many people keep telling me that loving the enemy is a difficult thing, but I do think that it is more difficult to hate one's enemy to the point of death. I am sure of one thing: you make more profit if you are courageous enough to love your enemy. If you hate your enemy, you will not do without the consequences of your hatred, which work reflexively.

ACKNOWLEDGMENTS

Thank you, God, for the unconditional love you have bestowed on me and for all the blessings I have received to this day.

My heartfelt gratitude to my parents for instilling the values of gratitude and faith into me and for all the sacrifice they accepted for me. I would like to thank Father Claude Simard, former senior priest of Kirarambogo Parish for his advice; the whole congregation of the Rogationist fathers, especially Father Arturo Mele, as I am convinced that members of this religious family played a crucial role in my life; Professor Gianfranco Basti of the Lateran University for his advice whenever I went to him; Bishop Ignazio Cannavò, former archbishop of Messina; and his successor, Archbishop Calogero La Piana for their understanding; Mr. and Mrs. Di Pietro, who always welcomed me as their own child in the family; Laura, her brother Carlo, and their friends for their frequent invitations for relaxation with their groups; the following priests: Achille, Filippo, Francesco Pati, Osa, Tindaro, and Cesare for their material, psychological, and spiritual support; the community of the Venturini fathers: Valentino, Angelo, Alberto, Maurizio, and Domenico for their support when I had just lost almost my entire family; Antonio, a trader in Barcellona Pozzo di Gotto, and his wife for compassion in difficult moments; Francesco Compagnoni, former dean of the Faculty of Social Sciences, St. Thomas University; and his successor, Helen Alford, for their beneficial good advice; and the community at the Center for Educational Orientation, particularly Don Francesco Pedreti and Maria Bianchi.

Many thanks also to Dr. Vincent Biruta for advice and assistance when I first returned to Rwanda; Dr. Emile Rwamasarabo, Professor Chrysologue Karangwa, former chairman of the board of directors of the University Teaching Hospital of Rwanda, for their understanding; François Mukuru Ntaganda for his advice in editing this book; Jean Damascène Gatera for technical advice in sending manuscripts; my brothers: Alexandre, Alexis, and Godefroid for sharing the heritage from Father; and finally, my wife, Marie-Claire, and my children, Davina and Anaïs, for their understanding and constant love.